Aboriginal Peoples

Aboriginal Peoples

Toward Self-Government

Edited by Marie Léger

Translated by Arnold Bennett

Montréal/New York
London

BLACK ROSE BOOKS No. X216
Hardcover ISBN 1-551640-11-2
Paperback ISBN 1-551640-10-4

Canadian Cataloguing in Publication Data

Main entry under title:
Aboriginal peoples: toward self-government

Translation of: Des Peuples enfin reconnus.
Includes bibliographical references.
ISBN 1-551640-11-2 (bound)
ISBN 1-551640-10-4 (pbk.)

1. Indigenous peoples—Latin America—Politics and government. 2. Indigenous people—Legal status, laws, etc.—Latin America. 3. Indians of Central America—Legal status, laws, etc. 4. Indians of South America—Legal status, laws, etc. I. Léger, Marie, 1952– .

E65.P4813   1994   980'.00498   C94-900627-0

Cover Design: Rasa Pavilanis

Mailing Address

BLACK ROSE BOOKS
C.P. 1258
Succ. Place du Parc
Montréal, Québec
H2W 2R3 Canada

BLACK ROSE BOOKS
340 Nagel Drive
Cheektowaga, New York
14225 USA

Printed in Canada
A publication of the Institute of Policy Alternatives of Montréal
(IPAM)

Contents

Acknowledgments

On behalf of the Centre d'études et de documentation d'Amérique latine, I wish to thank the International Centre for Human Rights and Democratic Development, Peace and Development, the Confédération des syndicats nationaux and the Secretariat for Native Affairs, which believed in this project and contributed financially to its achievement.

I also wish to thank CUSO, especially Don Cockburn for maintaining faithful contact with Colombia and Gilio Brunelli for his invaluable assistance concerning Brazil. My thanks also to SUCO for facilitating contacts in Nicaragua and to the Duiren Kuna youth organization for its warm and competent reception.

Gilles Rivet handled most of the translation into French and correction of the original Spanish texts, Tony Kwan translated part of the chapter on Colombia, Maria-Filomena Smith and Gilio Brunelli looked after translation from Portuguese to French, and Nancy Thede, Pierre Beaucage and Louise Chicoine shared their talents and skills. Without them, this book would never have seen the light of day.

Preface

by Marie Léger[1]

The idea for this book was born in 1992, when Canada, Québec and the First Nations were engaged in their constitutional wrangling. Even though the agreement reached at that time by their representatives did not win popular support, the Canadian political universe was changed nonetheless.

With the 1990 Oka crisis and the energetic opposition of the Cree to Hydro-Québec's projects, Quebecers had become aware that the pleasant folklore surrounding Québec's first inhabitants was outdated.

It would henceforth be necessary to admit that the Mohawks, the Cree, the Innu and other indigenous peoples are part of our present and will never settle for a place in museums, reservations or history books. This reality still provokes misunderstanding, fear, mistrust and anger. How can our territory be shared with a small group of people claiming to be the legitimate owners of the forests we want to exploit? How can we tolerate autonomous governments within our very borders? How should we react when they talk about their sovereignty?

What is often disregarded is that these questions are not only springing up in Québec or Canada. They are being asked everywhere in the Americas and even at the United Nations. Dialogues are engaged in different ways, conflicts erupt and initial solutions are implemented. The entire continent is in ferment. Peoples whom we had only read about in anthropology texts are now speaking up before parliaments in their native apparel, going to Geneva to cry out that they still exist and that their children want a future. People whom the Canadian, Panamanian and other governments wanted to become citizens like any others are refusing the fate that had been reserved for them.

At the Centre d'études et de documentation d'Amérique latine (CEDAL), we were struck by the resemblance of certain questions and reactions, but above all by the strength of the aspirations of indigenous or aboriginal peoples everywhere in the Americas: they all want protection for the territories on which they depend and respect for their way of life. They affirm that human diversity is a source of wealth and that political institutions should consider and preserve it.

As in Canada, the First Nations of Latin America are seeking constitutional recognition. In Nicaragua, Colombia and Brazil, significant changes have been made to basic laws; in Panama, the Kunas enjoy partial government autonomy. However, constitutional guarantees, although essential, do not mean that life is becoming easier in concrete terms. Tragedies sometimes intrude between constitutional formulas and everyday life. In Brazil, the massacre of Yanomami children, women and men in August 1993 was undoubtedly terrible, but it is not the only example. It is a reminder that the recognition of peoples whom Euro-Americans hoped would remain silent and despoiled of their land is not achieved without difficulty.

The purpose of this book is to bring together experiences which can fuel reflection. Authors from the three Americas responded to CEDAL's invitation. Others generously provided us with analyses and information.

Chapter 1 discusses indigenous rights from an international perspective. Pierre Lepage's history recalls that the First Nations of the Americas have long sought recognition from the international community and describes the main steps in this quest. Ted Moses then explains why the recourse to international bodies was necessary. Alejandro Morgado Zacarias and Herlinda Zacarias Hernandez discuss the application of Convention 169 of the International Labour Organization in the Mexican context.

The following chapters analyze certain Latin American constitutions from the perspective of the recognition they grant to native peoples. These serve as beacons for what is "possible." Whether in the case of multiethnic and regional governments as in Nicaragua, native territories as in Brazil or territorial governments as in Colombia or Panama, different approaches try to respond to the same requirements: recognition of ethnic diversity, a territorial base and governmental autonomy.

Analyzing different situations, the National Organization of Indigenous Peoples of Colombia, Marie Léger, Marlene Larocque, Aiban Wagua, Beatriz Perrone-Moisés and Paulo Machado Guimaraes propose a range of current responses to a very American emergency: the redefinition of the relationship between Amerindian peoples and the descendants of Europeans.

Without such a redefinition, we will continue to be deprived of part of our memory, part of the knowledge which belongs to this continent. And we will continue to be ignorant of the powder keg on which we are seated. This book is an attempt to understand where the change begins, through real experiences in political realignment.

Marie Léger

Note

1. Marie Léger is a sociologist and political scientist. A member of the *Centre d'études et de documentation d'Amérique latine* (CEDAL), a Montréal organization founded in 1976, she is responsible for issues concerning native peoples of Latin America. She headed the group which edited this book and personally wrote the chapters dealing with Nicaragua and Panama. She signs this preface on behalf of CEDAL.

Chapter 1

The Long Struggle for International Recognition

Indigenous Peoples and the Evolution of International Standards: A Short History

by Pierre Lepage[1]

In the past few years, indigenous political organizations have been criticized for making skilful use of international forums, including the United Nations (UN), to launch inappropriate attacks on the reputation of the various countries in which they live. This is seen as a new activist strategy, a new way to promote their own cause and acquire artificial and inordinate political clout.

The first part of this text demonstrates that there is nothing new about recourse to international bodies. Indigenous peoples have used this for a long time, and their presence at the United Nations has followed a long progress over the past two decades. Contrary to the prevailing impression, the presence of indigenous peoples largely results from initiatives taken by the United Nations itself.

It is true, however, that until the 1970s, the door of the United Nations was systematically closed to indigenous peoples. Despite the anticolonialist current which prevailed in the 1950s and 1960s, an entire facet of the colonial problem remained untouched. There was no question of interfering with what was considered to be strictly the internal business of a sovereign State. So what was the source of the reversal which, in the near future, could well lead to the adoption by the United Nations General Assembly of a Universal Declaration on the Rights of Indigenous Peoples?

The first diplomatic missions

The first international recourses of indigenous peoples took the form of appeals, petitions and requests to the imperial authorities of the various colonial powers. Starting in the 18th century, several requests were addressed to the British Crown and several ambassadors of the indigenous peoples visited London.

In 1710, four sachems of the Five Nations Iroquois Confederacy set sail for England to meet Queen Anne. They asked for missionaries and especially for military assistance against the French who posed a growing threat. This first visit, however, was fully encouraged by the colonial authorities of New York and New England, who saw this as a very good way of consolidating their alliance with the Five Nations. The latter had suffered huge losses because of their loyalty to the British.[2]

In 1730, seven Cherokee chiefs also visited England, where they concluded a treaty of peace and friendship with King George II. In 1762, another Cherokee delegation met King George III, just after the British conquest of New France.

Then came the turn of the famous Mohawk war chief, Joseph Brant. Having remained loyal to the British after the American Revolution, he visited England several times to defend his nation's cause. Dissatisfied with the promises of Canadian land he would obtain in compensation for lands lost in New York State, Brant visited London on two occasions. Pleading his cause to the British government and before the king, he finally obtained lands in the Grand River region of Ontario, near Brantford. Joseph Brant's grandfather was one of the four sachems who had visited England in 1710.

A major controversy soon developed about the land title granted to the Six Nations near Brantford. Joseph Brant's youngest son, Chief John Brant, also visited England in 1821-1822, with the mission of obtaining a final settlement of his nation's claim to title and sovereignty over these lands.[3]

In the same period, after exhausting all recourses to the local colonial authorities, the Huron Grand Chief Nicholas Vincent and three other chiefs of the Jeune-Lorette Hurons also decided to visit London, seeking a favourable decision in the dispute over the Sillery seigneury lands. They met King George IV on April 7, 1825. He received them very politely and promised to take their request into consideration. There were no new developments, however, and they had to make a new appeal to the local authorities.[4]

More recently, in 1906, a famous chief in British Columbia, Joe Capilano, headed a Squamish delegation to submit a petition to King Edward VII, after getting nowhere with a request to the local authorities. A large part of the Squamish lands had been designated for colonization without obtaining their consent. The Squamish delegation invoked the fact that their rights to these lands had never been ceded under any treaty.[5]

The history of the Nishga Indians in British Columbia also shows a long series of territorial demands dating from the turn of the century. After unsuccessfully demanding from the Ministry of Indian Affairs that their land rights be recognized prior to any sale or concession by the Province, they resorted to a new strategy. Having collected about $500 from their members and supporters, they decided in 1913 to retain a British law firm to present their case to the King of England and the Empire's highest court, the Privy Council. They were bitterly disappointed when their petition was rejected.[6]

These few examples clearly show that, on most occasions, the British authorities hesitated or even refused to intervene in the internal policies of the British North American colonies. As long as the different Indian nations constituted a strategic military force, the British Crown received them with great consideration, seeing them as a good means to consolidate its alliances to maintain the colony.

However, things changed with the end of the colonial wars. Amerindian ambassadors who set sail for London could not hope for anything more than an audience. At most, the monarch or the representatives of the British government could promise to use their influence. The settlement of these disputes was left to the discretion of the local authorities.

It should be noted, however, that the hope of obtaining a favourable hearing from the Crown or the Parliament in London has persisted to this day. In 1979, over three hundred Indian chiefs visited London, at their expense, to oppose the repatriation of the Canadian Constitution. They feared that this process would reduce their rights as recognized by the British Crown in the famous Royal Proclamation of 1763. In 1981, Alberta Indian chiefs met with the Queen of England and the British Prime Minister. After a somewhat cold reception, they nevertheless filed a petition with the High Court of Justice, affirming that the judicial responsibility for treaties concluded with the British Crown had never been transferred to Canada. They lost their case, but their initiative won them an invitation from the Canadian government to participate in the constitutional discussions specifically dealing with protection of their ancestral or treaty rights.

The Iroquois Confederacy at the League of Nations

The creation of the League of Nations in 1919 aroused new hopes. At least one petition has remained famous, that of Chief Deskaheh, a Cayuga from the Six Nations Reserve in Ontario. In 1923 and 1924, Deskaheh made a determined attempt to have the League of Nations and the Permanent Court of International Justice hear the case of his small nation. His aim was to have the Iroquois recognized as a sovereign nation.

Like others before him, he began with a visit to England, in 1921. To affirm his nation's sovereignty, he carried a passport issued by the Iroquois Confederacy.[7] This was a new approach. He then asked the British authorities to intervene on behalf of his people in a dispute with the Canadian government over Iroquois independence from Canadian laws, including the Indian Act, which the federal government was trying to impose. He recalled the terms of certain treaties and his nation's indestructible loyalty to its alliance with the British during the colonial wars. His effort was wasted. The embarrassed British authorities refused to intervene in what they considered to be Canada's internal affairs.

In 1922, Deskaheh visited Washington to meet the *chargé d'affaires* of the Netherlands and inform him that his nation wished to appeal to the Queen.[8] He invoked the very first alliance and the very first peace and friendship treaty concluded between the Iroquois Confederacy and a European nation, in the Hudson Valley in the mid-18th century. Deskaheh's plea impressed the Dutch Foreign Minister, who agreed to forward the Iroquois Confederacy's petition to the Secretary General of the League of Nations, although he avoided taking a position on the substance of the dispute. This decision immediately provoked a diplomatic incident between the Netherlands and the Dominion of Canada. But Deskaheh had acted perceptively, since under the League of Nations system, and under its successor, the United Nations, only a member State could address a request to the Assembly or to the International Court of Justice in The Hague. These were iron-clad rules, and no individual was allowed to take such measures.

The Canadian government replied swiftly. It declared that the Six Nations' claims to constitute an organized and self-governing people were absurd. It then announced that it would never tolerate the intrusion of another government into its domestic affairs. The Secretary

General of the League of Nations immediately intervened. To stifle this source of tension before it could hatch, he offered the Netherlands two options: either to inform the League of Nations Council officially of its intention to withdraw its request, or to send the document to the ten Council members purely as information, which would result in no reaction and put an end to the request. The Netherlands chose the second option. The affair nevertheless earned the Netherlands an official protest from Great Britain at this unqualified and unacceptable intrusion into the internal affairs of Canada.

In an attempt to rekindle the affair, Deskaheh paid a direct visit to Geneva in September 1923. He would remain there for over a year. The Six Nations Council, supported by the members of the Workers Committee, raised $5,000, a colossal sum in those days, to support its ambassador's mission.[9]

This time, Deskaheh, assisted by a lawyer, addressed his petition to the Secretary General of the League of Nations, invoking Article 17 of the organization's Charter. Article 17 concerned disputes between member States and non-member States.[10] According to Deskaheh, he was seeking international arbitration in a conflict between the government of the Six Nations Iroquois Confederacy and the governments of Britain and Canada, both members of the League.

Since the Secretary General refused to intervene unless a member State was a party to the request, Deskaheh embarked on a diplomatic offensive and obtained the support of four States: Estonia, Ireland, Panama and Persia. This was a great victory. These countries asked the President of the Assembly to place the question on the agenda, but technically it was too late to intervene, as the session of the League of Nations Assembly was ending. The issue had to wait another year.

In the meantime, stimulated by the support of the four countries' representatives, Deskaheh pursued his diplomatic offensive. He increased his number of speaking engagements and won the sympathy of non-governmental organizations. The success of his initiatives, according to some observers, were largely attributable to his qualities as an orator and his personal charisma.[11]

The simultaneous response of the Canadian and British governments was virulent: a diplomatic counteroffensive. In a declaration distributed to the members of the League of Nations at the Council meeting of March 1924, the Canadian government rejected any claim of the Six Nations to constitute a State. It declared this claim to be frivolous and without foundation. The Six Nations Indians, the Canadian government said, were British subjects residing in Canada. It then invoked the fact that they were governed by the Indian Act, which provided for a process of emancipation allowing them to acquire the status of Canadian citizens.[12]

The counteroffensive did not stop there, however. While Deskaheh was busy in Geneva, the Canadian government destabilized the Six Nations by using a dissident faction within the community. The faction in question had been demanding for several years that political leaders be elected, as provided in the Indian Act which the federal government was seeking to impose.

Thus, on the basis of an inquiry into the political situation on the Six Nations reserve, entrusted to a certain Colonel Thompson who claimed the existence of a group of agitators calling for separation as a justification, the government, without even consulting the population, ordered that elections be held. These elections took place on October 21, 1924 by order in council, under the supervision of Lieutenant-Colonel Morgan and officers of the Royal Canadian Mounted Police. This opened the door to declaring Deskaheh incompetent to represent his nation and without the authority to be its spokesman. For some, this interference by the Canadian government constitutes the worst historical injustice ever committed against this community.[13]

In the meantime, the diplomatic counterstrike by Canada and Great Britain continued. The representatives of the four countries favourable to Deskaheh's cause were called to order by their respective governments and had to cease all "intrusion into Canadian domestic affairs." Disappointed, Deskaheh returned home, but had to live in exile in the United States, where he died the following year. He nevertheless succeeded in embarrassing the League of Nations. Despite his remarkable initial diplomatic success, he finally failed, and it is appropriate to ask whether the failure of his mission definitively compromised future contacts between Amerindian peoples and international bodies.[14] Indeed, could they hope for anything more than to be classified as "ethnic minorities" by diplomatic circles?

It is hard to know whether other indigenous groups, outside of Canada, ever tried to be heard by the League of Nations. A Maori chief named Ranta also went to Geneva in 1924,[15] in the hope of being heard by the League of Nations, but without success. Did he encounter Deskaheh during his odyssey? No information is available.

The Iroquois Confederacy knocks at the door of the newly established United Nations

The creation of the United Nations in 1945 seemed to offer a little more hope. The Charter constituting the United Nations, adopted at the San Francisco Conference, contains promising provisions. The signatory States proclaimed their faith not only in the equality of human beings but also in that of great and small nations. The necessity of developing "friendly relations among nations based on respect for the principle of equal rights and self-determination of peoples" is presented in the Charter as one of the purposes of the United Nations.[16] The Charter also included a chapter full of hope for colonial territories, Chapter XI. The member States recognized as a "sacred trust" their obligation to favour the well-being of the inhabitants. In particular, they had to ensure respect for their cultures, encourage their advancement and see to it that they were treated justly and protected against abuses. The States had an explicit obligation to help these peoples develop self-government and to "assist them in the progressive development of their free political institutions." It is interesting to note the disappearance of the term "colony" itself. Henceforth, the term "non-self-governing territories" would be used. There would be no more colonizers or colonized, but administrators and people under administration.

These great principles obviously would remain a source of inspiration for many peoples seeking freedom and dignity. The indigenous nations of the Americas would be no exception. In 1945, an Iroquois delegation sought to be heard at the San Francisco Conference, where many States had assembled to adopt the founding Charter of the UN. This delegation, following in Deskaheh's footsteps, maintained the hope of obtaining a seat at the great table of nations.[17] However, this approach did not produce the desired result.

It was also in the mid-1940s that two great political movements took shape among the indigenous nations of Canada. In the western provinces, the North American Indian Brotherhood (NAIB) was created in 1944, on the initiative of British Columbia Squamish chief Andrew Paul. In the East, the North American Indian Nation Government was established in 1945, at the instigation of Jules Sioui, a Lorette Huron. An Algonquin, William Commanda, would become the first Supreme Chief.

These great movements would both seek an attentive ear within the newborn UN. In 1953, the NAIB dispatched an Indian delegation to United Nations headquarters in New York. They were received by John Humphrey, the Canadian head of the Human Rights Division, who informed them that they would have to address their complaints to the Canadian government.[18] The NAIB's approach was therefore rejected. The same attempt was made by Sioui's movement. We note with interest that the text of the proclamation of the North American Indian Government refers explicitly to the San Francisco Charter in the following terms:

> The human rights adopted by the world charter under the United Nations General Assembly cover all world humanity without exception. That law gives us the same rights as any other nation. Let us be united to be known as a true nation.[19]

Seeking to assert its international identity, the North American Indian Government adopted its own Indian Act[20] in 1947. However, this assertion of government autonomy would have a price. The organization's Secretary-Treasurer, Jules Sioui, found guilty in 1949 of inciting Canadian Indians to rebellion, was sentenced to a two-year prison term. This judgment was overturned on appeal.

The history of these numerous petitions and just as numerous disappointments is far from over. We know, for example, that the UN has regularly received complaints from indigenous individuals or groups alleging violations of their fundamental rights.[21]

In 1947, the Commission on Human Rights paradoxically decided that it could not receive complaints related to human rights. It would limit itself to the promotion and development of international standards.[22]

It was only in 1967, with the adoption of Procedure 1235, that individuals and organizations could submit complaints. However, only non-governmental organizations (NGOs) accredited with the UN could do so after being assured that all internal recourses had been exhausted.

The determination of the Iroquois Confederacy was utterly remarkable under the circumstances. A delegation had already attempted to be heard at the San Francisco Conference in 1945. In 1949,

Iroquois turned up again for the inauguration of construction of the United Nations headquarters in New York.[23]

But it was in 1958 that the militant action of the Iroquois Confederacy entered a new phase. That year, along with the Micosukee of Florida, it officially recognized Fidel Castro's revolutionary government. In exchange, Castro personally invited the two nations to visit Cuba.[24] During this trip, the Indian delegations hoped to obtain the Cuban government's support for their admission to the UN as sovereign and independent nations. But even though recognitions of sovereignty were exchanged, this initiative did not produce the desired result.

Just before the trip, one of the delegation's leader, Wallace Mad Bear Anderson, had made contact with indigenous groups in Mexico and Central America, seeking to create a pan-American movement.[25] In 1959, Hopi representatives also visited the UN and established ties with the Iroquois Confederacy.

It is no surprise that during the same period, the Kahnawake Band Council in Québec (formerly Caughnawaga) also addressed the United Nations as members of the Six Nations Confederacy, to protest against the expropriation of part of the reserve for construction of the St. Lawrence Seaway.

After several failures before the local courts, Chief Matthew Lazare of Kahnawake sent two successive petitions, in 1959 and 1960, to the UN Commission on Human Rights and the Secretary General. Obviously, given Commission's limited terms of reference, these efforts yielded no concrete results, despite the hiring of a lawyer specializing in international law.[26]

The door of the UN closes

Nevertheless, from the start of its activities, the UN was marked by the anticolonialist thrust of Chapter XI of its Charter. The aim was the disappearance of colonial domination through the generalized application of right of peoples to self-determination. It must be noted that the decolonization process which followed effectively enabled many dependent peoples and millions of individuals to acquire a new dignity. This, however, was not the case for the many indigenous peoples whose territories could not be considered overseas territories, that is, geographically separate from the metropolis or the mother country. Because of the application of the famous "salt water" theory, an important part of the colonial question would escape any international control. At its first session, in 1946, the United Nations General Assembly established a list of 74 non-autonomous territories. These essentially were overseas colonies and protectorates. Thus, only the territories included in the 1946 list and a few others, added in 1960, would become non-autonomous territories, within the meaning of Chapter XI of the UN Charter.[27]

Was the situation of indigenous peoples, whose territories could not be considered geographically separate, taken into account? According to Professor Douglas Sanders, Belgium had put forward a thesis, at the time, whereby the provisions of Chapter XI would also apply to indigenous populations living in contiguous territories or constituting enclaves within certain States. Belgium maintained that the fact of limiting the application of the anticolonial provisions solely to overseas territories and protectorates constituted an injustice for other peoples. The Belgian thesis was rejected, however. In fact, Central and South American countries and other former colonies strongly opposed it. Some of them, which had just acquired their independence, feared that the Belgian thesis would pose a new threat to their sovereignty and territorial integrity.[28]

During the 1960s, the movement for liberation of peoples and achievement of independence accelerated. To give it new impetus, the United Nations General Assembly in 1960 adopted the Declaration on the granting of Independence to colonial countries and peoples (UN Resolution 1514). The contents of this important document were particularly explicit. It constituted an unprecedented condemnation of colonialism and a moral recognition of the validity of the passionate desire of all dependent peoples for freedom.

Colonialism "in all its manifestations" was described as the denial of fundamental human rights in the following terms:

> The subjection of peoples to alien subjugation, domination and exploitation constitutes a denial of fundamental human rights, is contrary to the Charter of the United Nations and is an impediment to the promotion of world peace and cooperation.

The generalized application of the right of peoples to self-determination was also reaffirmed:

All peoples have the right to self-determination; by virtue of that right they freely determine their political
status and freely pursue their economic, social and cultural development.

While peoples of differing race and ethnic origin were kept in a
state of dependence on other peoples, the struggle against
colonialism was recognized as an essential means to attack racism
and racial discrimination. However, despite the apparent generosity
of this declaration and the hopes that it inevitably aroused, one
short paragraph would limit its application considerably. This paragraph affirmed that "any attempt aimed at the partial or total
destruction of the national unity and the territorial integrity of a
country is incompatible with the purposes and principles of the
Charter of the United Nations."[29]

The day after the adoption of the Declaration on the granting of
independence to colonial countries and peoples, the General Assembly adopted a new resolution (Resolution 1541) which definitively settled the question. Henceforth, member States would be obliged to
transmit information to the UN on colonial territories only in the case
of a territory geographically separate and ethnically or culturally distinct from the country which administers it.[30]

Under this principle, the requests of many indigenous peoples of
the Americas and other continents would be ruled out of order. The
door of the United Nations was shut. From now on, the fate of these
peoples would be determined within the sacred sphere of a State's internal affairs.

Beyond this principle, certain common prejudices of the time
were conveyed by the UN. Thus, many indigenous peoples were considered as not "sufficiently evolved" or as not having achieved the
level of development deemed essential to exercise the right to self-
determination. The capacity of some of these peoples to administer
themselves was doubted, or they were considered too small to constitute States. This view of human societies pervaded several official
UN reports. It stemmed more from a unilinear evolutionism (from
simple to complex) rather than from an egalitarian vision of peoples
and nations, great or small. This certainly explains, at least in part,
why some indigenous peoples were unable to obtain the necessary
support to claim their right to self-determination.

The forgotten people of international law

It therefore is no surprise that, until recently, no major United Nations document has contained provisions referring specifically to the situation of indigenous peoples.[31] It is also easy to note, in reading the official publications distributed until the late 1960s by the United Nations Information Service,[32] that the question of the fundamental rights of indigenous peoples, for all practical purposes, did not exist.[33]

There are several reasons for this situation. First, the decolonization process was confined to the narrow framework of geographically separate overseas territories, while the situation of other indigenous peoples fell within the realm of a State's internal affairs. Yet according to Article 2.7 of the Charter, "nothing ... shall authorize the United Nations to intervene in matters which are essentially within the domestic jurisdiction of any state."

Secondly, until the 1970s, the dominant current of opinion at the UN undoubtedly was the assimilator-integrator model. To consolidate the Nation-State, different governments favoured the promotion of assimilationist cultural policies. There was scarcely any place for cultural pluralism, the enhancement of ethnicity or the expression of diversity. To borrow the expression of anthropologist Michael Elbaz, there were "citizens to be created."[34] This generalized current largely explains the tardiness of the United Nations in developing international standards suitable for ensuring adequate protection for indigenous populations collectively[35] and minorities in general.

Thirdly, the nature of the human rights advanced by the UN's member States was primarily individualistic. This approach went hand in hand with the assimilator-integrator tendency, and it is no exaggeration to say that this connotation was no threat to States. As one author put it, the real beneficiary of human rights was undoubtedly the individual.

> The major international instruments adopted in this field to date, such as the Universal Declaration of Human Rights and the two United Nations Covenants on Human Rights, clearly indicate this: it is the human being, the human person, any individual, to use the terminology of these instruments.[36]

The individual character of human rights thus relegated collective rights — the rights of groups and minorities in general — to second place, or rather, it should be said, to last place. For John Humphrey, former director of the UN's Human Rights Division, the international instruments reflected the profound belief of the member States that "if the rights of everyone are protected without distinction as to race, sex, language or religion, nothing else needs to be done."[37]

Finally, the absence, until the mid-1970s, of specifically indigenous non-governmental organizations also makes it easier to understand the shortcomings of the international instruments. NGOs accredited with the UN have always played an important role in the mechanics of human rights. Their presence acts as a counterweight to State power. Furthermore, they make an essential contribution to the formulation of new international standards.

An inadequate recourse and a two-edged sword

Recent decisions of the UN Human Rights Committee clearly show the inadequacy of recourses when collective rights are involved.[38] In a dispute between the Lubicon Lake Crees and the Government of Canada, Chief Bernard Ominayak presented a brief to this Committee in 1984. He affirmed, in the name of his community, that the Canadian government was violating Article 1 of the International Covenant on Civil and Political Rights, which formally recognizes a people's right to self-determination, its right to dispose of its wealth and natural resources and its right not to be deprived of its own means of subsistence. Under an optional protocol to which Canada adheres, individuals who believe themselves to be victims of a violation of one of the rights set forth in the Covenant are allowed to address the Human Rights Committee.

In its March 1990 decision, the Committee rejected the complaint of the Lubicon Lake Crees on the right to self-determination in the following terms:

> The question whether the Lubicon Lake Band constitutes a "people" is not an issue for the Committee to address under the Optional Protocol to the Covenant. The Optional Protocol provides a procedure under which individuals can claim that their individual rights

have been violated. These rights are set out in part III of the Covenant, Articles 6 to 27 inclusive.[39]

Although the complaint was filed under the right to self-determination, a collective right, the Committee agreed to analyze certain grievances in the light of an individual right. This right, as set forth in Article 27 of the Covenant, is stated as follows:

> In those States in which ethnic, religious or linguistic minorities exist, persons belonging to such minorities shall not be denied the right, in community with the other members of their group, to enjoy their own culture, to profess and practice their own religion, or to use their own language.

The Committee finally concluded, in the following terms, that there was indeed a violation of a right under the Covenant:

> The historic inequalities mentioned by the party State, and certain more recent facts, threaten the way of life and the culture of the Lubicon Lake band and constitute a violation of Article 27 as long as they have not been eliminated.

Under this same Article 27, Sandra Lovelace, a Malecite from the Tobique reserve in New Brunswick, won her case with the Human Rights Committee in 1981. Lovelace denounced the Indian Act, which caused women to lose their Indian status when they married non-Indians. They were therefore forbidden to reside on the reserve. However, Indian men who married non-Indian women did not suffer the same fate. Sandra Lovelace therefore argued that there had been violations of several rights, including the right to equality provided in Article 26 of the Covenant.

She lost her case because Canada had not yet ratified the Covenant at the time that she lost her Indian status. However, the Committee found the petition to be allowable under Article 27. The loss of Indian status deprived her, according to the Committee, of her individual right to have her own cultural life in common with the other members of her group.[40]

The impact of these two decisions on the Government of Canada, whose reputation was stained internationally, allows one to conclude that these were impressive victories. These victories also had major importance if one considers that these petitions were only possible to the extent that all internal recourses had been exhausted. But this approach was a two-edged sword. These two decisions confirmed, in effect, that in the current interpretation of international law, indigenous peoples could hope for nothing more than to be recognized as ethnic minorities within a State.

ILO Convention 107 fosters assimilation

We have said that no major UN document mentioned the specific situation of indigenous peoples. Notwithstanding this, we must cite Convention 107, entitled Convention concerning the Protection and Integration of Indigenous and other Tribal and Semi-Tribal Populations in Independent Countries. It was adopted in 1957 by the International Labour Organization (ILO), an autonomous intergovernmental agency affiliated with the UN. The title of the Convention is explicit: its goal is integration.

To measure the meaning and scope of Convention 107, it is appropriate to take a brief look at the ILO's mandate. Founded in 1919, the ILO's primary objective was to institute an International Labour Code to serve as a model for national legislation. The object of the ILO's work was oriented to social justice: abolition of forced labour, union freedom, elimination of discrimination in employment, fair and healthy conditions of employment, etc.

It is in this capacity that the ILO has long been interested in the situation of indigenous workers in the countryside, seeking to eliminate the barriers to their integration into the national economy or to protect them from exploitation. Nevertheless, the Convention has instead served as an alibi for assimilation.

> The main purpose of the government policies envisaged by Convention 107 was to find effective measures and means to ensure the complete integration of this labour force distinct from the majority society. Today, with the evolution of social attitudes to these groups, we can observe that this emphasis on their complete integration was an invitation to

governments to impose a forced assimilation of these peoples.[41]

In reality, the Convention would have few effects. In all, only 27 countries ratified it, the majority of them in Latin America. Canada and the United States never signed it. This document was often criticized for its paternalistic and assimilationist approach. It is therefore no surprise that the people primarily concerned generally rejected it. The ILO itself admitted that it was obsolete and undertook its revision. In 1989, the ILO adopted Convention 169, the preamble to which openly declares *that it is appropriate to adopt new international standards on the subject with a view to removing the assimilationist orientation of the earlier standards.*[42]

Convention 107 nevertheless contained some interesting provisions. It had seen the importance of considering customary law and indigenous modes of social control. It had also understood the necessity for recognizing the right of collective and individual ownership by indigenous peoples of their traditional lands, as well as their mode of use as consecrated by custom.

Entering the UN by the service entrance

A renewed interest in issues concerning indigenous peoples was evinced at the UN in the early 1970s. How can this be explained?

There are three main points of entry to the UN. First are the member States, which occupy a dominant and often exclusive position. At this level, the indigenous question is considered as interference in the internal affairs of States. Next are international non-governmental organizations accredited with the UN, which play an important role. However, no indigenous organization was part of this group until the mid-1970s. The new point of entry was therefore that of "special studies" conducted by experts working for the Sub-Commission on Prevention of Discrimination and Protection of Minorities. It is important to note that the Sub-Commission's members are primarily experts. They sit as individuals and not as representatives of States.

Particularly concerned about racial discrimination in the mid-1960s, the United Nations simultaneously adopted the Declaration and the International Convention on the Elimination of any Form of Racial Discrimination. A series of studies were conducted in this vein. One of them focused on discrimination in the political, economic, social and cultural fields. Entrusted to Hernan Santa Cruz, it was made public in 1971. Part of this general study was devoted to the situation of indigenous populations. However, it is important to note that it only expressed the viewpoint of governments.[43]

However, the Santa Cruz study expressed doubt about the value of the so-called measures for *protection of indigenous populations*, and the value of organizations created by States for this purpose. Santa Cruz wondered whether Indian Affairs agencies simply hindered the development of indigenous communities or even oppressed them, instead of protecting them. Upon completing his study, the author recommended that the competent United Nations agencies proceed with a "complete and exhaustive study of the problem."

This recommendation finally led to a wide-ranging study on discrimination against indigenous populations. The author, José R. Martinez-Cobo, entitled his report *Study of the Problem of Discrimination against Indigenous Populations.*[44] The Martinez-Cobo report was made public one chapter at a time, after more than ten years of work. The last section of the report, finally published in 1987 in summary form, contained the conclusions, proposals and recommendations.

The Martinez-Cobo report is impressive both for the scope of the fields covered and for the innovative and trenchant character of its analysis and recommendations. Thus, the creation in 1982 of the Working Group on Indigenous Populations is the direct result of one of the report's recommendations. The study also made people aware of the importance of seeking the viewpoint of those primarily concerned. The United Nations Economic and Social Council (ECOSOC) also subsequently fostered the emergence of many indigenous nongovernmental organizations. The criteria for accrediting organizations and giving them a voice within the UN's many agencies therefore would be applied flexibly.[45]

The Martinez-Cobo study stands totally apart from the policies previously adopted by States regarding their indigenous populations. While the Hernan Santa Cruz study, only a little while earlier, still favoured the integration of indigenous peoples, the Martinez-Cobo report innovated:

> Pluralism, self-management, self-government, autonomy and self-determination within a policy of ethnic development ... appear to be the formula called for by the times in which we are now living and to do justice to

the aspirations and desires of indigenous populations, which for so long have been subjected to interference and imposed conditions of all kinds.[46]

It should be noted that international conferences have proliferated and have served as a privileged source of information for the author of this study.

The birth of indigenous NGOs

Non-governmental organizations play a significant role within the complex system of the United Nations and its affiliated agencies. Their presence serves as a counterweight in a system dominated, we must never forget, by States. The Commission on Human Rights might never have existed without the pressure exerted in 1945 by the NGOs present at the San Francisco Conference.[47] Their determining influence on the contents of several international declarations and conventions must be acknowledged. Access to international forums is limited, however, to non-governmental organizations meeting certain criteria and which have first obtained official consultative status, particularly from ECOSOC.

It was necessary to wait for the mid-1970s to see the emergence of specifically indigenous NGOs. The movement, born in North America, took shape in two ways.

In 1969, a mobilization of indigenous organizations in Canada gave birth to the National Indian Brotherhood, which quickly realized the necessity of addressing international bodies. The Brotherhood then tried to obtain consultative status at the UN, which was granted in 1975.

This was a first. That same year, under the presidency of George Manuel, the Brotherhood held a five-day meeting in Port Alberni, British Columbia, with indigenous representatives from the following 19 countries: Canada, United States, Australia, New Zealand, Norway, Sweden, Finland, Denmark (Greenland), Argentina, Bolivia, Colombia, Ecuador, Guatemala, Mexico, Nicaragua, Panama, Paraguay, Peru, Venezuela and Hawaii. The delegates from Brazil and Chile had been unable to obtain visas to leave their countries. The Bolivian and Guatemalan representatives insisted that no publication be distributed which would allow them to be identified.[48] This meeting led to the creation of the World Council of Indigenous Peoples.

This organization initially functioned through the accreditation obtained by the National Indian Brotherhood of Canada, then obtained its own in 1981. Bringing together indigenous peoples from several continents, it would continue to have major influence, serving as an umbrella organization for many indigenous groups seeking to be heard by the UN.

During the same period, the American Indian Movement was created in the United States. Its international branch, the International Indian Treaty Council, was founded in 1974. This second umbrella group won consultative status at the United Nations in 1977 and would have a determining influence on later events. Among others, the International Indian Treaty Council would play a central role in the holding of the first major United Nations Non-Governmental Organization Conference on Discrimination Against Indigenous Populations in Geneva, in 1977. This conference would be perceived as a first breakthrough in a field which until then had fallen purely within the realm of a State's internal affairs. Sixty indigenous organizations would adopt a first great common declaration entitled: Draft Declaration for the Defence of the Indigenous Nations and Peoples of the Western hemisphere. This document attempted to summarize all indigenous demands and would have a determining influence. It took its inspiration from international standards on human and national rights, expanding them to ensure adequate protection for the collective existence and cultural and territorial integrity of these peoples. The 1977 Declaration would serve as a backdrop for the preparation of the Fourth Russell Tribunal on the Indians of the Americas, meeting in Rotterdam in 1980. On this occasion, fourteen cases of violations of the fundamental rights of various indigenous peoples would be brought to the attention of the international community.

In this short history, it is important to mention the supporting role of the Indian Law Resource Center. Founded in the United States in 1978, this organization obtained consultative status at the UN. Among its noteworthy achievements was the production of a handbook on international recourses and procedures for indigenous organizations, entitled *Indian Rights — Human Rights*.[49] The Indian Law Resource Center would help channel many complaints to international agencies. It therefore would play a crucial role in mastering the complex legal mechanisms of the UN and its affiliated agencies.

In this rapidly growing movement, the contribution of organizations supporting the cause of indigenous peoples cannot be ignored. In particular, we should mention Survival International and the International Work Group for Indigenous Affairs (IWGIA). The latter organization, headquartered in Copenhagen, was founded in 1968 by anthropologists, who had witnessed the many crimes and abuses committed against indigenous populations in South America.

Links were established through many international conferences and new indigenous NGOs emerged. They took advantage of meetings to inform each other and initiate international proceedings and recourses. From time to time, they would set up international observer missions.

In South America, Indians initially associated with the World Council of Indigenous Peoples, created their own international organization in 1980, the *Consejo Indio de Sur-America* (CISA) and obtained consultative status in 1987. The indigenous peoples of the Amazon basin, living in eight different countries, in turn created their own representative organization in 1984 in Lima, Peru. The *Coordinadora de las Organizaciones Indigenas de la Cuenca Amazonica* (COICA) symbolized the birth of a new pan-Amazonian identity. And this organization wished to become an equal participant in the Geneva meetings.[50]

In the North, the Inuit, some of whose delegates had been present at the creation of the World Council of Indigenous Peoples in 1975 in Port Alberni,[51] founded the Circumpolar Inuit Conference in 1977 in Barrow, Alaska. There as elsewhere, mobilization was accelerated by events. The announcement in 1975 of vast prospecting projects by major oil companies in the Beaufort Sea was perceived as a serious threat to the Northern environment. The Inuit of Canada, Alaska (United States of America) and Greenland (Denmark) therefore created their own international NGO, which obtained consultative status in 1987. A few years later, they were joined by the Inuit of the USSR.

Other organizations emerged and developed their distinctive identities. Such was the case of the Four Direction Council, bringing together activists from the Cheyenne, Lakota, Micmac and Innu nations, who met in Geneva in 1983. The Council would obtain its consultative status in 1988-89. The Innu branch of this organization, the *Innu Kanantuapatshet*, mainly campaigned in Europe against low-level military flights in Labrador and on the North Shore of the

St. Lawrence. These activists would hold many meetings with delegations from different countries and explore the possibility of being recognized as a national liberation movement. They thus sought a more direct access to the privileged forums of the UN. This approach did not have the expected success.

Finally, the progress of the Grand Council of the Crees (of Québec) is worth special mention. Its presence on the international scene dates back to 1981 when it participated, in Geneva, in the International Non-Governmental Organization Conference on Indigenous Populations and the Land Question. The Crees recalled the "conditions of extreme constraint" under which the James Bay and Northern Québec Agreement had been signed in 1975. They benefited from their European visit to ask the World Health Organization to investigate the problems of health services in the James Bay region.

Over the years, the Cree representatives have acquired definite credibility in their interventions at international bodies. Initially sponsored by the World Council of Indigenous Peoples, the Crees obtained their own consultative status in 1981. This nation thus would become the only one to have its own consultative status; the other NGOs cover several nations.

It is important to note that, at a seminar on the "Effects of Racism and Racial Discrimination on the Social and Economic Relations Between Indigenous Peoples and States,"[53] it was a Cree, Ted Moses, who was designated as reporter to the Commission on Human Rights. Unanimously chosen by the representatives of fifteen governments and ten indigenous NGOs, he became the first member of an indigenous people to fill this prestigious position.

Working Group on Indigenous Populations

The creation in 1982 of the Working Group on Indigenous Populations was probably the most significant factor in opening the United Nations to the situation of indigenous peoples. Considered particularly vulnerable, these peoples henceforth could rely on their own UN body. The Working Group, created by the Sub-Commission on Prevention of Discrimination and the Protection of Minorities, was entrusted with a twofold mandate. At its annual meetings held in August, the Group first reviewed new facts about discrimination and the rights of indigenous populations. It then quickly took on the difficult task of preparing new international standards capable of assuring them of adequate protection.

Many governments at first feared that this new body, even deprived of any judicial or quasijudicial power, would be transformed into a forum for complaints which finally would only serve to attack States publicly. The Working Group on Indigenous Populations did indeed display an openness unprecedented in the history of the United Nations. As we have mentioned, ECOSOC was intentionally flexible in accrediting indigenous NGOs. In turn, the Working Group on Indigenous Populations, wishing to encourage expression by the people primarily concerned as much as possible, agreed to hear many representatives from indigenous organizations which the UN had not yet accredited.

In the annual review of new facts concerning these populations, it was inevitable that denunciations of abusive practices, all kinds of mistreatment and even atrocities in certain countries would be exposed to public view. Governments nevertheless understood that this forum was also available to announce positive developments, particularly constitutional changes and experiments in internal autonomy.

However, the Working Group did not lose sight of its task of drafting a Universal Declaration on the Rights of Indigenous Peoples. Over the years, standards were defined. A first complete draft was tabled in 1988. In 1989, the Working Group agreed to replace the expression "indigenous populations" with "indigenous peoples." Finally, despite the opposition of representatives of many governments, including Canada, a clear affirmation of the right to self-determination suddenly appeared in the revised document of 1991.

It can easily be asserted that the Working Group on Indigenous Populations, even though it is at the bottom of the UN organizational structure, has gained enviable popularity. Its influence is currently felt at every level of the UN and its affiliated agencies. Its recommendation to conduct a study on treaties and other types of agreements between governments and indigenous peoples was followed. The mandate for this study was entrusted to a special reporter, Miguel Alfonso Martinez. One recommendation also led to the creation of a voluntary fund to allow the various representatives of indigenous peoples to come to Geneva and participate in work sessions. Many ideas germinated as a result of recommendations by indigenous organizations which held preparatory sessions each year for the sessions of the Working Group. The fact that 1993 was declared the International Year of Indigenous Peoples originated in this process. Following the recommendation by many indigenous NGOs to create a position of High Commissioner for indigenous questions or international mediator in conflicts between States and indigenous peoples, the idea of international recourses made progress.

Towards official recognition

In the past ten years, we have seen the emergence on the international scene of a reality quite distinct from that of ethnic minorities. The Working Group on Indigenous Populations is the most obvious expression of this reality. In 1983, the General Assembly, the highest body of the United Nations, had already adopted a Programme of Action for the Second Decade to Combat Racism and Racial Discrimination. It invited the different States to adopt a series of measures likely to ensure the promotion and protection of the rights of indigenous peoples, under the title of *Measures for the promotion and protection of the human rights of persons belonging to minority groups, indigenous populations and peoples and migrant workers who are subjected to racial discrimination*. For the first time, though timidly, the expression "indigenous peoples" appeared in an official document adopted by this Assembly. The distinct situation of indigenous peoples was also accepted in the Convention on the Rights of the Child, ratified in November 1989. For the first time in an international agreement, a distinction was made between "minority groups" and "persons of indigenous origin." This formulation, though imperfect, was the result of pressure exerted by indigenous NGOs which, while awaiting recognition as peoples, did not want to see the expression "indigenous populations" entrenched.

This new ferment also led the ILO to do a thorough revision of its Convention 107, adopted in 1957 and considered obsolete. This process led to the June 1989 adoption of Convention 169, entitled Convention concerning Indigenous and Tribal Peoples in Independent Countries.

Convention 169 came into force in 1991, one year after two ILO members, Mexico and Norway, had ratified it.[54] It denoted tremendous progress in the recognition of the fundamental rights of indigenous peoples in all fields, if only through the elimination of previous standards oriented to integration and assimilation. However, even though this Convention refers to "indigenous peoples," paragraph 3 of the first article limits its scope. This paragraph clearly indicates that the use of the term "peoples" should not be interpreted as "having any implications as regards the rights which may be attached to this term under international law."

The revision process was also a source of great frustration for indigenous NGOs which could not participate directly in the work. The ILO's specific tripartite structure gives an equal voice to representatives of governments, unions and management.

* * *

Hopes are now invested in the draft Universal Declaration on the Rights of Indigenous Peoples. While the use of the term "indigenous peoples" and the recognition of the right to self-determination seem to be established for the experts of the Working Group responsible for drafting, no presumption can be made as to the final result. In the final analysis, it will be governments that will be called upon to adopt this document. Nevertheless, one certainty remains: this Declaration will generate new collective rights, as Convention 169 has already done.

This short history shows that the evolution of the question of indigenous peoples on the international scene is the result of a long process. It is not a spontaneous reaction to noisy aboriginal activism. The strength of this movement does not only depend on the effective evolution of international law. It has already materialized in the political pressure exerted on many countries where indigenous peoples live. This largely explains why several governments have already initiated radical reforms.

"A new partnership" was the theme chosen to mark the International Year of Indigenous Peoples. The Chairperson of the Working Group on Indigenous Populations, Erica Irene Daes, told the General Assembly that "this means bringing an end to the racism, colonialism and paternalism being suffered by indigenous peoples and the beginning of a new era marked by participation, self-government, autonomy and self-determination."[55]

Seeking Justice at the International Level

by Ted Moses[56]

Indigenous peoples face a legal conundrum when they attempt to understand and assert their human rights. Although they find themselves in their own homelands, living in the places they and their ancestors have never left, they are confronted by a legal system that is not theirs. Yet none of the indigenous peoples have any recollection that they have ever revoked or abrogated their own system of law, or that they have ever consented to have their rights determined by European or colonial legal systems.

This is a most peculiar situation. How is it that I, a Cree, whose ancestors have lived in the Cree Territory of James Bay for at least 5,000 years, find myself and my people suddenly subject to the laws of States that were only established a few hundred years ago?

Consider also the basis of the legal systems that these States have created. These systems are invariably erected on the principle that their laws have exclusive jurisdiction, that no prior system of law existed or exists, and that all authority rests with the State.

What place do the indigenous peoples have within such a system of law? The answer is that the indigenous peoples do not really exist within these systems at all. These legal systems, and we can use Canada, Australia or Brazil as examples, not only displace all prior legal jurisdictions, they also deny that there ever were or are other systems of law besides their own.

These legal systems start with the assumption that the sovereign territory of the State was either vacant (*terra nullius*) or that the people who lived there were so primitive as to lack any modicum of social organization and thus the capacity to govern themselves.

Whether the result of ignorance or abuse of authority, this is the fundamental and grounding historical principle upon which law in the Americas is established, and upon which the contemporary sovereignty and legal authority of States is based and asserted. No exercise in modern anthropology or comparative law has ever been able to disabuse the constituted legal authority of its absolute belief that it has dominion and jurisdiction over the indigenous peoples.

This then defines our status within States, our contemporary standing, so to speak; and it is to this constituted legal authority that we have to turn to be informed of our rights.

It comes as no surprise then, that a legal authority constituted on such specious grounds, an authority that denies our existence or at least our legal competence and capacity to act, would have very little interest in recognizing our rights. And this is indeed the case. Indigenous peoples, we are told, have no title to their lands. We have certain rights as individuals. In Canada, and in many other States, these are rights of diminished legal competence, essentially the rights of children. We are, in other words, wards of the State. The State is our fiduciary, charged constitutionally to protect us and our lands. The State acts on our behalf, or at least, that is the stated legal principle.

When, under certain circumstances, the indigenous peoples do manage to escape this patronizing relationship, they find themselves in another equally demoralizing situation. They are condemned to be classified as "minorities," divested of their collective rights and their political, cultural and historic identity. They find themselves, ironically, in exactly the same legal category as the most recent immigrants to their own land. They enjoy no recognition of their original ownership of the land. Their system of law, their language, and their cultural and spiritual ties to the land are dissolved forever.

Consider also the real nature of the fiduciary relationship between the indigenous peoples and the State. The indigenous peoples, who were initially in possession of all of the land and resources and were their own masters, find themselves now a dispossessed people, with minuscule plots of land "reserved" for their use. The somewhat larger tracts of land originally reserved for their use have gradually been alienated under the so-called trusteeship of the State. The indigenous peoples find themselves generally the most disadvantageous group in the States where they live. And this holds true whether they live in developed or developing countries, and regardless of the quality of democracy they enjoy.

I have made this brief outline of our legal and historical relationship with States in order to place my basic thesis within a suitable context. The quest of the world's indigenous peoples to have their rights as peoples recognized only begins to make sense once the facts are examined within this context.

The indigenous peoples have not, in reality, been the beneficiaries of the fiduciary trust held by the States; they have rather been the victims of that trust. A malicious guardian has the ability to do great harm to his ward, for it is in the very nature of the relationship that the ward's diminished legal capacity frustrates his ability to exercise the necessary remedy. This is not an analogy for the relationship between indigenous peoples and States — it is the exact status of that relationship.

The most essential questions arise when indigenous peoples seek legal remedies. If we seek redress through the courts, we find our every move vitiated by the pervasive authority of the State — the State which erects the laws, enforces the law, defines our rights, defends the "national interest," prosecutes the laws, renders judgement, and acts as the court of last resort.

It can hardly surprise us if indigenous peoples' rights have been steadily diminished under such a system; nor is it inconsistent that States cite the supremacy of the "rule of law" whenever indigenous peoples object to the injustice of the present arrangements. The rule of law invariably serves the purposes of the State, and was promulgated, please recall, without the participation or knowledge of the indigenous peoples.

The injustice in the present arrangements rests in the fact that indigenous peoples are held captive by a system of laws inimical to their welfare and best interests. The administration of justice would better be served by reference to a system of law that would avoid the obvious conflict of interest between the State and the indigenous peoples.

This is why indigenous peoples have finally turned to the international community. At the national or domestic level, indigenous peoples confront a situation where their own laws have been arbitrarily and unilaterally replaced by an entire other system of law. This law, domestic or "municipal" law, is unfortunately founded upon obvious racial principles of superiority and supremacy.

The remedy, I believe, is to be found in the international community, outside of national or municipal legislation and jurisdiction. Indigenous peoples must demand that their rights be respected under international law, as subjects of international law. It is for this reason that we must examine recent developments at the United Nations.

In August, the United Nations Sub-Commission on Prevention of Discrimination and Protection of Minorities received a draft document from a working group that was appointed over eleven years ago. That working group, known as the Working Group on Indigenous Populations, was given the responsibility to draft international human rights standards for the protection of the rights of indigenous peoples. In other words, it was charged with the task of writing new international law on indigenous rights.

This task has proved somewhat difficult, not because it was difficult to devise human rights standards that should apply to indigenous peoples, but rather because some States have continued to insist that their own domestic laws should define the rights of indigenous peoples. A few States, such as Brazil, India, Canada and China, do not want the rights of indigenous peoples to be recognized under international law. They do not want the subject of indigenous peoples to be "internationalized." They do not want indigenous peoples to be recognized as "subjects of international law."

These States claim that jurisdiction over indigenous "populations," they refuse to identify indigenous peoples as "peoples," is exclusively domestic, and they accuse the United Nations of violating their sovereignty and interfering in their internal affairs whenever the issue of indigenous rights is raised at the international level.

Canada, and certain other States that are historic abusers of the rights of indigenous peoples, also raise other objections: Canada claims that recognition of our rights as peoples under international law will encourage us to seek independence and assert some kind of national aboriginal sovereignty. Applying this rationale, Canada, Brazil and others have been working against the setting of new international human rights standards for indigenous peoples at the United Nations and other international forums. These States argue that their own domestic laws already provide adequate protection, and that nothing should be done at the international level that would require these States to amend their own laws.

Notwithstanding the difficulties and delays that these objections have caused, historic developments have nevertheless taken place. In August of this year, the Working Group on Indigenous Populations completed the Draft Declaration on the Rights of Indigenous Peoples and agreed by consensus to have it submitted for technical revision during the coming year. Next year it will be tabled for comment by the participants at the Working Group, and will be submitted to the Sub-Commission on Prevention of Discrimination and Protection of Minorities.

For eleven years the Working Group consulted with indigenous peoples, United Nations member States, non-governmental organizations, intergovernmental organizations, United Nations agencies, academics and experts to assist in the preparation of the Draft Declaration. The Grand Council of the Crees has participated at the United Nations in this exercise since 1981. In 1987, the Grand Council of the Crees was granted consultative status by the Economic and Social Council of the United Nations.

It is important to bear in mind that the Draft Declaration as submitted by the members of the Working Group on Indigenous Populations is not a draft prepared by the indigenous peoples themselves. Rather, it is a document produced by a formally constituted United Nations body, a working group attached to the Commission on Human Rights, one of the commissions of the Economic and Social Council.

Because the Draft Declaration represents the findings of United Nations "experts," who have engaged in extensive and in-depth consultation and research, the Draft Declaration comes into existence with a particular level of credibility as well as intellectual and moral authority. It is by no means a final document; it is not a declaration but simply a draft of a proposed declaration. However, it does take into consideration the concerns expressed by the member States, and it does largely reflect the concerns raised by the indigenous peoples.

It is also useful to note that the very existence of such a document of the United Nations is in itself a recognition of the legitimacy and appropriateness of treating indigenous human rights questions at the international level. When we consider that the International Labour Organization has already approved two international conventions on the Rights of Indigenous and Tribal Peoples (Conventions 107 and 169), and that the United Nations has held numerous seminars, expert and technical meetings on indigenous rights issues, we begin to understand that indigenous rights questions are finding their place at the international level. The recent declaration by the General Assembly of an International Year of Indigenous Peoples, and the regular consideration by the Sub-Commission of the agenda item titled "Discrimination against indigenous peoples," firmly establishes indigenous peoples as subjects of international law. I believe that the United Nations will not step back from this position.

Nevertheless, the Draft Declaration on the Rights of Indigenous Peoples has a long way to go in the United Nations system. It must still be approved by the Sub-Commission; it must then be approved by the Commission on Human Rights, and only then will it be sent to the Economic and Social Council. Once these approvals have been obtained, it will be submitted to the Third Committee of the General Assembly, and finally to the General Assembly itself.

Our concern, then, is that the Draft Declaration will survive this process, and that the human rights of the indigenous peoples, so painstakingly described in the draft, do not themselves become victim to the States that have victimized the indigenous peoples. In particular, the indigenous peoples are most concerned about politically motivated amendments that might be put forward by States to prevent our international rights from being recognized.

For the indigenous peoples, this means that we must work to prevent Canada, Brazil, India, China and other like-minded States from weakening the international recognition of our rights as indigenous peoples, a recognition that is now within reach after hundreds of years of injustice, denial and dispossession.

Although it is not possible in this article to examine all of the provisions of the Draft Declaration, it will be informative to examine what I consider to be the most important of all:

> Indigenous peoples have the right of self-determination. By virtue of that right they freely determine their political status and freely pursue their economic, social and cultural development.

This article establishes the guiding principle of the entire Draft Declaration: that indigenous peoples may freely choose their own form of government, and that they are free to determine how they conduct economic, social and cultural development, that they are free to determine how they will relate to States.

This provision parallels the provisions found in the International Covenant on Civil and Political Rights and the International Covenant on Economic, Social and Cultural Rights, both part of the International Bill of Rights. The international Covenants recognize that "all peoples" have the right of self-determination. Article 1 states that "by virtue" of the rights of self-determination, all peoples are free to enjoy the wealth of their land and its resources, and that peoples are not to be "denied their own means of subsistence."

Do not fail to note that these rights are already embodied in international law. Under the international Covenants the right of self-determination is directly and permanently linked to ownership and control of land and resources, benefit from the wealth of the land, and at the very least the right to utilize the land to maintain subsistence. Yet these are the very same rights which have been most consistently violated.

The indigenous peoples need these protections, which already have the force of international law, and which gain elaboration and specificity in the Draft Declaration on the Rights of Indigenous Peoples. The indigenous peoples must have recourse to a neutral jurisdiction, and the Draft Declaration gives shape to the possibility, the hope that the international community will recognize and protect the rights of indigenous peoples.

The Draft Declaration recognizes the dignity of the indigenous peoples, our right of self-determination, our right to land, our right to control resources, our right to practise our own religions, our right to manifest our own cultures, our right to our own identity.

Have no illusions. This Declaration would be very difficult to enforce. In its present form it would be non-binding. But it would establish an appropriately high standard, set a principle and place the administration of justice for indigenous peoples on a level with other principles of international law and the aspirations of the indigenous people themselves.

The Implementation of an International Convention in Mexico

**by Alejandra Morgado Zacarias
and Herlinda Zacarias Hernandez[57]**

Convention 169 of the International Labour Organization (ILO) has had the force of law in Mexico since 1991, in all of its States and throughout the territory of the Republic. However, despite the rights that it recognizes and the protection it advances, there is still little knowledge of this Convention.

Mexico's indigenous peoples traditionally have had little legal and cultural protection because of circumstances particular to judicial practice in this country. Even though Convention 169 has force of law, the indigenous peoples do not yet benefit from any of the advantages provided by the various legal steps involved. The Convention therefore has gone unnoticed in practice, both for the indigenous peoples at whom it specifically aims and for the political and judicial authorities.

Thus, three years after the Convention came into force, no lawsuit based on this document has yet been initiated and no legal opinion has yet been issued by the Supreme Court.

This particular situation exists despite the new Article 4 of the Mexican Constitution, which took effect after the Convention's signing and which guarantees indigenous rights. This article reads as follows:

> The composition of the Mexican nation is multicultural and sustained originally by its indigenous peoples. The law shall protect and favour the development of their languages and cultures, their usages and customs, their resources and their specific forms of social organization. It shall guarantee the indigenous peoples real access to the judicial organs of the State. In judgments and lawsuits of an agrarian nature to which the indigenous peoples will be party, their judicial practices and customs shall be taken into account, according to the terms established by law.

Despite this guarantee, the Convention has not been invoked by the indigenous peoples either as a reference or as a means of defending their rights. Neither has it been put forward in the various branches of Mexican law.

However, beyond this initial assessment of the enactment and limited application of the Convention, it must be noted that something truly new has been introduced in Mexican law. An extremely important legal precedent has been created by the reform of Article 4 of the Mexican Constitution, which recognizes the rights and customs of indigenous peoples on the basis of the ILO Convention.

This addition to the country's fundamental law constitutes a remarkable recognition of the nation's multiethnic and multicultural composition. Once the legal category expressed in the Convention has been inserted in the Constitution and converted into guarantees for the rights arising from the ethnic origin, customary practices and inherent cultures of indigenous peoples, it acquires a legal dimension in Mexican law which is absent from Convention 169. This is the first explicit recognition of indigenous rights in Mexican legislative history. In this sense, constitutional entrenchment is rooted in Convention 169 and requires regulation to render it enforceable. Such regulation is currently under discussion at the Union Congress.

Furthermore, legislative jurisdiction over this matter primarily belongs to each State of the Mexican federation, since there are at least 56 ethnic groups distributed throughout the country, each with its own characteristics. In this regard, the enactment of Convention 169 serves as a reference point for the ethnic groups of each State, to foster the adoption of local laws adapted to their needs and cultural characteristics. The new Constitution of the State of Veracruz, adopted in 1992, moves in this direction. Indigenous peoples represent a substantial percentage of the population of this State and there are many conflicts. The constitutional changes have led to the reform of secondary laws, such as penal law, in order to recognize the rights and customs of this State's ethnic minorities. At this time, nongovernmental organizations supporting the indigenous peoples are proposing other reforms of civil and municipal law. Similar experiences are under way in other Mexican States.

All of this indicates that Convention 169 has influenced Mexican legislative bodies, in contrast with the few changes in legal practice concerning all of the controversies in which indigenous peoples are embroiled.

It is important to emphasize the considerable weight of this Convention in the national legal order. Thus, Article 133 of the General Constitution of the Republic, which establishes the hierarchy of laws governing access to justice and its administration, obliges judges to apply the treaties or conventions concluded by the executive of the Union and ratified by the Senate. Article 133 reads as follows:

> This Constitution, the laws of the Union Congress which emanate therefrom and all the treaties arising therefrom, which are concluded or in the process of being concluded by the President of the Republic with the approval of the Senate, will be the supreme law of the entire Union. *The judges of each State shall cause the said treaties, laws and Constitution to prevail, notwithstanding any contrary provisions which may exist in the Constitutions or in the laws of the different States.*

Thus, on the constitutional level, the Convention may be applied by all courts and judicial bodies. Despite this, no recourse has been made to the Convention either as a means of defence or as a source of legal solution. This situation is paradoxical for Mexico, given the large number of trials to which indigenous communities are subjected, in most cases under very disadvantageous conditions.

Given its disuse as a legal instrument, the Convention is little known to ethnic groups, particularly rural indigenous communities who are constantly marginalized by the national legal system and who lack defenders and lawyers to protect them. It is also little known to the courts, especially those of a penal nature, where indigenous people are often charged with various offenses. They are held in detention without any assurance that they will have a fair trial, the services of a translator or interpreter, or the assistance of anthropological experts to help them establish the truth regarding the acts of which they are accused.

Despite the constitutional reform, there are few real procedural guarantees that judges will apply the reform in their decisions or the trials under their jurisdiction.

On the other hand, the Commission and the related Mexican laws are discussed in the social organizations and civil and cultural associations of indigenous people, as well as in the groups that support them, where the land claims or cultural demands of the different ethnic minorities are channelled. These groups and associations are even proposing draft legislation to give regulatory force to the recent constitutional guarantee granted by the general law. They are insisting on different concepts found in the ILO Convention, since it is considered to be more advantageous to them.[58]

All of these groups have launched far-reaching debates in coming to the defence of indigenous rights under the law and the constitutional order. In some cases, they have instilled lawmakers with enough backbone to promulgate or amend legal standards affecting indigenous customs, which previously had only considered positive Mexican law.

At present, associations are organizing legal education workshops with the support of lawyers, anthropologists and traditional indigenous authorities or their representatives. They are also spreading information about the legal usefulness of Convention 169 under the Constitution of each State, in order to defend indigenous legal rights and interests before the competent courts.

However, these efforts have proved to be unsatisfactory because national programs which provide this type of legal aid, such as the National Native Institute, the first to disseminate Convention 169, have not managed to reach all of Mexico's fifty-six ethnic groups or to force the lower courts to observe this legislation on every occasion.

Because of this situation, there is a general need for a firmer commitment by the Mexican government. This government has signed the Convention and must disseminate it more widely to the authorities, organs and courts of first instance, where the lack of legal protection for indigenous people is most flagrant. They often appear before courts other than their traditional ethnic courts and under circumstances of social and cultural inequality.

As a next step, the Mexican government must inform the indigenous peoples of the legal framework which, under national and international law, provides them with legal instruments or protection to guarantee the preservation and development of their identity and their material and cultural heritage.

Notes

1.   Pierre Lepage is an anthropologist responsible for indigenous issues at the Education Branch of the *Commission des droits de la personne du Québec* (Quebec Human Rights Commission).The opinions expressed in this text are those of the author and do not represent the official position of the *Commission des droits de la personne du Québec*.
2.   John G. Garratt, The Four Indian Kings, Public Archives of Canada, 1985.
3.   Carolyn T. Foreman, *Indians Abroad 1493-1938*, Norman, University of Oklahoma Press, 1943, p. 99.
4.   Marguerite Vincent, "Un siècle de réclamations de la Seigneurie de Sillery par les Hurons (1791-1896)," *Recherches amérindiennes au Québec*, vol. VII, nos 3-4, 1978, p. 22.
5.   E. Palmer Patterson II, *The Canadian Indian: a History Since 1500*, Toronto, Collier-Macmillan Canada Ltd., 1972, p. 169.
6.   Nishga Tribal Council, *Citizens Plus. The Nishga people of the Naas River Valley in Northwestern British Columbia. Nishga land is not for sale,* (revised edition), New Aiyansh, Nishga Tribal Council, 1980, p. 11.
7.   Akwesasne Notes, *Deskaheh. Iroquois Statesman and Patriot,* Akwesasne, Six Nations Indian Museum Series, 1978, p. 8.
8.   Joëlle Rostkowski, "The Redman's Appeal for Justice: Deskaheh and the League of Nations," in Christian F. Feest (ed.), *Indians and Europe,* Herodot, Rader Verlag, 1987, p. 438-440.
9.   Akwesasne Notes, op. cit., p. 4.
10. Rostkowski, op. cit., pp. 440-441.
11. Akwesasne Notes, op. cit., pp. 11-12.
12. Rostkowski, op. cit., pp. 448-449.

13. Sally M. Weaver, "Six Nations of the Grand River, Ontario," in William C. Sturtevant, *Handbook of North American Indians, Vol. XV: Northeast,* Washington, North Smithsonian Institute, 1978, p. 533.
14. Rostkowski, op. cit., p. 436.
15. Douglas Sanders, "The Re-Emergence of Indigenous Questions in International Law," *Canadian Human Rights Yearbook/Annuaire canadien des droits de la personne,* 1983, University of Ottawa, p. 14.
16. *United Nations Charter and Statutes of the International Court of Justice,* New York, United Nations Information Service, 1945.
17. Sanders, op. cit., p. 14; and Ursula Kuster, *From Identity to Resistance: North American Indians' International Politics,* paper submitted to "Langues vivantes étrangères (LVE — Civilisation)" and to Charles V, Université de Paris VII, Jussieu, Paris, 1989, p. 62.
18. Sanders, op. cit., p. 14.
19. The North American Indian Nation Government, *Proclamation,* June 21, 1945. This quotation has been edited to eliminate the many typographical errors found in the original document.
20. The North American Indian Nation Government, *The Second Session of the North American Indian Nation Government,* September 15, 16 and 17, 1947, Wolverine Hotel, Detroit, 12 pp.
21. Douglas Sanders, "Aboriginal Rights: The Search for Recognition in International Law," in Boldt and Long (eds.), *The Quest for Justice. Aboriginal Peoples and Aboriginal Rights,* Toronto, University of Toronto Press, 1985, p. 300.
22. Pierre Bosset, *The Enforcement of Human Rights by the Political Organs of the United Nations. A Critical Analysis,* thesis, University of Cambridge, 1989, pp. 53-56.
23. N'tsukw and Robert Vachon, *Nations autochtones en Amérique du Nord,* Montréal, Fides, Collection "Rencontre des cultures," 1983, p. 145; and Kuster, op. cit., p. 42.
24. *Encyclopedia of Indians of Canada, Vol. I,* Detroit, Scholarly Press Inc., 1977, p. 282.
25. Kuster, op. cit., p. 35.
26. Omar Z. Ghobashy, *The Caughnawaga Indians and the St. Lawrence Seaway,* New York, The Devin-Adair Company Publisher, 1961, pp. 113-120; and Richard C. Daniel, *A History of Native Claims Processes in Canada 1867-1979,* Research Department, Indian and Northern Affairs, 1980, p. 141.
27. United Nations, *Everyman's United Nations: a complete handbook of the activities and evolution of the United Nations during its first 20 years, 1945-1965,* New York, United Nations Information Service, 1968. Citation is from p. 460 of the French edition, *L'ONU pour tous.*
28. Sanders, op. cit., pp. 18-19.
29. United Nations, General Assembly 1960a: *Declaration on the granting of independence to colonial countries and peoples,* Resolution 1514.
30. United Nations, General Assembly 1960b: *Principles which should guide Members in determining whether or not an obligation exists to transmit the information called for under Article 73e of the Charter.* Resolution 1541.
31. The first major UN document which explicitly refers to indigenous peoples is the *Convention on the Rights of the Child,* adopted by the General Assembly in 1989.
32. United Nations, 1968, op. cit.
33. To be convinced of the absence of UN interest in the aboriginal question and the plight of indigenous peoples, it is sufficient to glance through an official publication distributed in 1968 by the United Nations Information Service entitled *Everyman's United Nations: a complete handbook of the activities and evolution of the United Nations during its first 20 years, 1945-1965.*

34. Presentation by anthropologist Michael Elbaz to the *Commission des droits de la personne du Québec*, as part of the staff training program in interethnic and race relations, May 26, 1993.

35. Margaret E. Galey, "Indigenous Peoples, International Consciousness Raising and the Development of International Law on Human Rights," *Revue des droits de l'homme*, vol. VIII, no 1, 1975, p. 24.

36. Jean-Bernard Marie, "Relations entre droits des peuples et droits de l'homme. Distinctions sémantiques et méthodologiques," *Annuaire canadien des droits de la personne 1988*, Centre de recherche et d'enseignement sur les droits de la personne, University of Ottawa, 1989, p. 194.

37. Cited in Galey, op. cit., p. 24.

38. On this subject, see Communication No. 167/1984: *Bernard Ominayak and Lubicon Lake Band v. Canada*, and Communication No. 197/1985: *Kitok v. Sweden*.

39. United Nations, Human Rights Committee, *Chief Bernard Ominayak and Lubicon Lake Band v. Canada*, Communication No. 167/1984, CLPR/C/38/D/167/1984, 1990, p. 32.

40. United Nations, Human Rights Committee, *Sandra Lovelace v. Canada*, Communication no 24/1977, 1981.

41. Michael Hudson, "Le statut juridique de l'Autochtone dans le droit international et le droit national — une perspective canadienne," in *Droit civil et droits autochtones, confrontation ou complémentarité?*, collection of papers presented to the Henri-Capitant Conference of April 12, 1991 at the Faculty of Law of the Université de Montréal, Association Henri-Capitant (Section Québec), June 1992, p. 168.

42. ILO, *Convention 169. Convention concerning Indigenous and Tribal Peoples in Independent Countries*, adopted by the International Labour Conference in Geneva, June 27, 1989, 24 pp. See Appendix I for excerpts from the Convention.

43. Henan Santa Cruz, *Racial Discrimination. Special Study on Racial Discrimination in the Political, Economic, Social and Cultural Spheres*, New York, United Nations, UNESCO, Sub-Commission on Prevention of Discrimination and Protection of Minorities, 1971, p. 157.For example, in revising its policies regarding indigenous populations, the Canadian government expressed its point of view as follows: "The Canadian government has indicated that its programs concerning Indians and Eskimos seek the quickest possible achievement of full participation in Canadian society, on the same basis as other citizens." (Translation of quotation from the French version of the report). In fact, the government was promoting the policy put forward in 1969 by the *White Paper* of Indian Affairs Minister Jean Chrétien. Since the point of view of those primarily concerned was not presented, nothing indicated that this apparently generous policy had been the object of unanimous opposition and unprecedented mobilization by Indian organizations throughout Canada. These saw this "alleged equality" as a clever assimilationist manoeuvre which denied their specific rights as the land's first occupants.

44. José R. Martinez-Cobo, *Study of the Problem of Discrimination Against Indigenous Populations. Volume 5. Conclusions, Proposals and Recommendations*, New York, United Nations, UNESCO, Sub-Commission on Prevention of Discrimination and Protection of Minorities, 49 pp.

45. Douglas Sanders, "The UN Working Group on Indigenous Population," *Human Rights Quarterly*, vol. II, no 3, August 1989, p. 419.

46. Martinez-Cobo, op. cit., p. 34.

47. Anne-Marie Panasuk, "Rompre le silence," *Recherches amérindiennes au Québec*, 1982, vol. XII, no 2, pp. 145-152.

48. Jim MacDonald, "Conférence des aborigènes," *Canadian Labour*, September 1976, pp. 27-28.

49. Indian Law Resource Centre, *Indian Rights — Human Rights. Handbook for Indians on International Human Rights. Complaint Procedures*, Washington, 1984, 129 pp.

50. Bernard Saladin D'Anglure and Françoise Morin, ""Nouveaux Mondes" indigènes et "Grands jeux" occidentaux dans les bassins amazoniens et circumpolaires," manuscript, 1988, pp. 25-28.

51. Macdonald, op. cit., p. 26.

52. Saladin d'Anglure and Morin, op. cit., pp. 33-35.

53. United Nations, Centre for Human Rights, *The United Nations Seminar on the Effects of Racism and Racial Discrimination on the Social and Economic Relations between Indigenous Peoples and States*, Geneva, 16-20 January 1989.

54. Alain Bissonnette, "Le droit à l'autonomie gouvernementale des peuples autochtones: un phénix qui renaîtra de ses cendres." in *Revue générale de droit*, Université d'Ottawa, Vol. 24, No. 1, 1993, p.17.

55. Erica-Irene Daes, *Statement by Prof. Erica-Irene Daes, Chairperson of the Working Group on Indigenous Populations before the Plenary of the General Assembly, 47th Session, on the Opening of the International Year of Indigenous Peoples*, New York, December 10, 1992, p. 6.

56. Ted Moses is the ambassador of the Grand Council of the Crees (of Québec) to the United Nations. In Geneva, he represents the Crees on the Working Group on Indigenous Peoples. He was the first member of an indigenous people to serve as a seminar reporter to the Commission on Human Rights.

57. Alejandro Morgado Zacarias and Herlinda Zacarias Hernandez are members of the Indian Peoples Support Group (GAPI) in Veracruz, Mexico. Mr. Morgado Zacarias is a lawyer and President of GAPI.

58. Excerpts from Convention 169 can be found in Appendix I.

Chapter 2

Regional Autonomy on Nicaragua's Atlantic Coast

by Marie Léger

A Distinct Society

Distinct by its history, Nicaragua's Atlantic Coast also stands out for its specific traditions, the diversity of the languages spoken in that region and the religion practised there.

The Atlantic Coast of Nicaragua takes up more than half of the nation's territory and contains major natural resources (mineral, forest and ocean products). It is now divided into two administrative regions: the Northern Atlantic Autonomous Region (NAAR) and the Southern Atlantic Autonomous Region (SAAR). Its population of about 300,000 accounts for 9.5 percent of the Nicaraguan total.

While Nicaragua's Pacific Coast was colonized by the Spaniards who exterminated or hispanicized the natives, the Atlantic Coast was marked by its relationship with Great Britain and Jamaica, and then with the United States. On the Atlantic Coast, the indigenous peoples were not exterminated. On the contrary, the Miskitos allied themselves with the British and repelled Spanish efforts to colonize them until the end of the 19th century. Suspicion of Spaniards, and thus of everything coming from the Pacific Coast, persists to this day.

Christopher Columbus passes through; the English stay

During his fourth voyage, in 1502, Christopher Columbus visited Cape Gracias a Dios, located to the north of the modern NAAR. But he only passed through. After this first contact, two expeditions explored the region but did not succeed in colonizing it or establishing a permanent settlement.

More than a century later, in 1631, a British company set up shop on Providence Island to grow tobacco and cotton and engage in trade. Labour was provided by slaves brought from Jamaica. This first European settlement only lasted ten years and was destroyed by the

Spaniards in 1641. It nevertheless marked the beginning of the slave trade and a long tradition of exchanges and alliances between the Miskitos and the English, first with buccaneers and then with colonists who gradually settled there. In 1747, there were about 1100 non-indigenous people on the Atlantic Coast.

Profiting from these contacts and alliances, the Miskitos obtained firearms. This could explain how they acquired a dominant position over the region's other ethnic groups.

The Miskitos and the representative of the British Crown in Jamaica regularly exchanged gifts as testimonies of friendship. Diplomatic relations were the responsibility of a Miskito chief whom the English appointed king. This individual signed a first official treaty with Great Britain in 1720. The Miskitos undertook to send 50 men to Jamaica to help the English fight Maroons, Blacks who had escaped from the plantations.

The Miskitos considered themselves to be a sovereign people and considered the English as allies. However, this did not prevent the British from granting rights to Miskito territory and exercising some control over its nationals. In the 18th century, they appointed a military superintendent for the Atlantic Coast without consulting their native allies.[1] From the British point of view, Mosquitia was subject to the colonial government of Jamaica. According to their respective logic, the Miskitos expected protection and the English expected support from their military allies.

Even after Great Britain recognized Spain's rights over the region in the Treaty of Versailles, signed in 1787, and most of the colonists had to emigrate to Belize, England's influence was maintained. However, the departure of the colonists allowed the emergence of a Miskito and Creole elite.

In 1821, after Spain's withdrawal from the region, a new stage began in the relationship between the two peoples.

> For the first time, the British government used the Miskito kingdom as a legal pretext to maintain a protectorate over the Atlantic Coast, against the will of the Central American republics which had just been born.[2]

It was at this point that competition between English and Americans intensified. Both countries wanted to build a canal between the Pacific and the Atlantic, which would pass through the Rio

San Juan, on the southern border of present-day Nicaragua. The Americans cosied up to the Nicaraguan government, while the English relied on their historical alliance with the Miskitos.

Between 1844 and 1894, a series of legal and political changes swept the Atlantic Coast. In 1844, the British Consul, Patrick Walker, declared that Mosquitia was a British protectorate, with Bluefields as its capital. This southward shift of the Miskito crown brought British interests closer to Rio San Juan, the maritime route envisaged for the future canal. The Miskito king, educated in Jamaica, moved with his circle to Bluefields, far from Rio Coco and Sandy Bay, where the Miskito population was concentrated. He would recruit his advisers mostly from the Bluefields Creole elite. From this time on, the influence of the Miskitos seems to have declined in favour of the Creoles.[3] The protectorate's new borders reduced the extent of the Miskito kingdom, which previously had stretched from Honduras to Panama.

In 1850, the Clayton-Bulwer Treaty defined Mosquitia as a political entity independent of Nicaragua. At the same time, Nicaragua and the United States were bound by a trade treaty. In 1860, the Treaty of Managua between England and Nicaragua recognized Nicaragua's sovereignty over the Atlantic Coast. However, it created the Mosquitia reservation, where it was provided that the indigenous peoples would govern themselves and all of the territory's other residents. However, this reservation did not include the entire traditional Moskito territory since its northern limit was Puerto Cabezas, excluding the entire native region of Rio Coco. In certain respects, the reservation possessed structures which the new Republic of Nicaragua did not yet have — its own currency, labour relations legislation, recognition of the necessity for free education and an import tax system. Although the reservation was under Nicaragua's authority, the autonomous government retained jurisdiction over natural resources.

According to historians, it was mainly the Creoles who profited from the newly created institutions,[4] while the Miskitos found themselves politically and economically marginalized.

Moravian brethren and American companies

The Miskitos have had contact with Europeans since 1631. However, they were not subjected to any massive attempt at evangelization until the mid-19th century, the few 17th century Spanish attempts having failed. The Miskitos have their own religious traditions, to which Afro-American elements have been added. However, in the mid-19th century, when the British were trying to keep their influence over the Atlantic Coast, the Consul General of the United Kingdom considered that the modernization of Mosquitia's political and social structures required the evangelization of its people. He believed that once they were educated and converted, they would agree more readily to engage in wage labour and integrate into a consumer market. Patrick Walker, who had worked on the signing of the Clayton-Bulwer Treaty, therefore tried to interest the Anglican Church in the evangelization of the natives, but without success. However, the Moravian Church[5] responded to Walker's appeal and established itself in Bluefields in 1849. It initially worked with the English-speaking Creoles before pursuing its mission to the Miskitos. Around 1880, the Moravian brethren began teaching the Bible in the Miskito language and there was a wave of mass conversions in Miskito communities between 1881 and 1883.

The Moravian Church, in the course of time, became a powerful institution on the Atlantic Coast. Favoured by the U.S. companies which dominated the economy in the latter half of the 19th century, it offered essential health and education services.

All of these changes coincided with the growing power of U.S. companies which, attracted by the abundance of natural resources, came to the region to exploit the forests and mines — especially gold mines — cultivate bananas and produce rubber. By 1890, 90 percent of the Atlantic Coast's trade was controlled by the United States. Companies such as the Nicaragua Long Leaf Pine Lumber Co. (NIPCO) exploited the best forests between 1945 and 1963 without any concern for reforestation. By the time NIPCO closed its doors, vast expanses of land had become unusable.[6]

This system of exploitation reached its apogee in the first half of the 20th century and began to decline in the 1950s. In the late 1920s, Sandino's guerrilla war had caused the departure of several U.S. companies from the Rio Coco region. During that period, the number of wage-paying jobs increased, without generating any integrated economic development. The U.S. companies organized production for export. They imported U.S.-manufactured products to Nicaragua but did not invest in the establishment of local industry. This was what was known as the "enclave economy." This form of exploitation depleted resources without creating a stable economic infrastructure. It introduced consumer goods to which the people became accustomed, but without developing the capacity to produce them. Finally, it consolidated the ethnic division of labour, confirming the Creoles in their role as a middle class and confining the indigenous people to seasonal manual jobs. The latter continued to live on agriculture for their subsistence and on wage labour to have access to imported products.

Despite this rather negative balance sheet in terms of development, many inhabitants of the Atlantic Coast remember the era of the companies as a period when jobs and imported goods were available.

From Zelaya to the Sandinistas

It was only at the end of the 19th century that the Atlantic Coast was reintegrated into Nicaragua (the Creoles use the word "overthrown"). President Zelaya's troops occupied Bluefields on February 11, 1894. The reservation authorities were dismissed from their posts and Spanish was decreed the official language. Resistance was organized but was unable to alter the course of events. A petition of 50 Miskito village headmen and 1800 Creoles asked Queen Victoria to intervene and prohibit forcible incorporation. The British would have preferred the voluntary integration of the Miskitos, as provided in the Treaty of Managua, but they did not intervene.

At the same time, a Nicaraguan military leader, Cabezas, embarked on an intensive diplomatic effort to convince the Miskitos to cede their rights. Since several Miskito communities had lived outside the boundaries of the reservation and under Nicaraguan authority since 1860, Cabezas' work was facilitated. On November 20, 1894, he managed to assemble the Miskito headmen, who signed a decree, in the presence of the U.S. Consul, ratifying their incorporation into the Republic. The decree exempted the Miskitos from taxes and military service, gave them the right to vote and allowed them some latitude in the management of local affairs. Nicaragua undertook to legalize land titles, grant at least the equivalent of 8 *manzanas* (1 manzana equals 0.7 hectares) per family living on the Atlantic Coast and allow the use of public lands for livestock.[7]

This legal integration and the disappearance of Mosquitia did not cause any abrupt changes for the people and the U.S. companies continued their operations. However, the arrival of *Mestizo* peasants from the Pacific Coast[8] and the hiring of Spanish-speaking Nicaraguans in the civil service gradually changed the human and social landscape. The Creoles were supplanted by Mestizos and the marginalization of the indigenous population became more acute. Nevertheless, these arrivals did not break the Atlantic Coast's isolation from the rest of the country.

In 1934, Atlantic Coast leaders complained to the central government about the abandoned state of their region. They even accused it of allowing the companies to do as they wished and of failing to respect the spirit of the incorporation decree, which provided for reinvestment of profits in the region's development.

During the 1950s and 1960s, under Somoza, a few attempts at economic integration triggered land disputes with Miskito communities, without really putting an end to their isolation. In the 1970s, an indigenous movement sprang up around the farming co-operatives of Rio Coco, which created ALPROMISU, one of the organizations which contributed to the founding of the World Council of Indigenous Peoples. The Sumus and the Creoles also created their own organizations around 1975.

When the Sandinistas took power in 1979, the Atlantic Coast was going through one of the worst economic crises in its history. Most companies had left the region, leaving behind obsolete equipment and depleted forest resources.

The new government wanted to deal with this situation, but it did so without taking the distinctiveness of the Atlantic Coast into account. In this sense, it seemed no different than the governments which had preceded it in Managua. Like them, it gave priority to declaring the integrity and indivisibility of Nicaraguan territory and confirmed Spanish as the official language. It nevertheless recognized the necessity of protecting and developing different forms of cultural expression; it guaranteed the communities ownership of the lands they had traditionally occupied (1981 declaration) and encouraged their participation in development agencies.

The Sandinistas' objective was social and economic modernization. They therefore planned their development strategy for the Atlantic Coast in the same way as for the Pacific Coast. Sandinista cadres were sent to the region and their bureaucratic behaviour was badly received.[9] The indigenous peoples and the Sandinistas negotiated for awhile, but the historical suspicion of the people of the Atlantic Coast hardened and differences degenerated. Accusations succeeded suspicions and negotiations gave way to armed conflict.

Some indigenous organizations allied themselves with the Contras, which the United States hastened to help, even though the opposition essentially focused on indigenous rights. Sandinista troops fought in the Rico Coco region and, in 1982, displaced 9,000 people after razing their villages for so-called national security reasons. In all, nearly 20,000 Miskitos were displaced or became refugees in Honduras when the war reached almost all communities. The region's rare infrastructures were damaged and international opinion was indignant at the fate of the indigenous populations.

In 1983, the Sandinista National Liberation Front (FSLN), officially acknowledging the importance of the ethnic question, began to change its attitude by declaring a general amnesty. It also admitted that indigenous combatants should not be likened to the Contras. It favoured the creation of an indigenous organization willing to co-operate with the government, created the National Autonomy Commission and committed itself to a bilingual literacy program. Starting in 1985, the situation changed: negotiations led to local ceasefires and the government allowed displaced persons to return to Rio Coco. Finally, consultations began between the different social groups on the issue of future autonomy. The official Statutes were ratified in October 1987.

Between integration and independence: autonomy

The history of the Atlantic Coast is different from that of the rest of Nicaragua. It has been defined over the centuries by its resistance first to the control of Spain and then to that of Nicaragua.

The existence of diplomatic relations between a Miskito king and the British Crown symbolized the equality of sovereign nations. Although this relationship changed over the years and the extent of the kingdom's territory was reduced radically in the 19th century, it nevertheless remains that there is no lack of legal evidence of special status, and even of independence. Even the forced integration of the Atlantic Coast into the Nicaraguan State included special provisions concerning the Miskitos.

The traditional inhabitants of the Atlantic Coast speak Creole English or indigenous languages, unlike those of the Pacific Coast. They are of the Protestant religion and their economy is linked to that of the Caribbean countries. History has made them a distinct society which has long enjoyed autonomous institutions. Many tendencies coexist among the peoples of the Atlantic Coast. However, the demand for autonomy or recognition of their sovereignty and ancestral rights brings them together, in that it is deeply rooted in their history and political practices.

The Sandinista government approached the problems of the Atlantic Coast without taking this historical dimension into account. The Sandinistas wanted to wipe out underdevelopment and poverty everywhere in Nicaragua. In their view, the resource-rich and underpopulated Atlantic Coast was indispensable to the country's future and development.

The Sandinista discourse on social justice, modernization, national unity and development was perceived as an additional step towards assimilation by the "Spaniards." Misunderstanding quickly degenerated into conflict and confrontation. The ethnic reaction, both of the indigenous peoples and of the Creoles concentrated in the Bluefields region, was exacerbated. Nevertheless, it was the Miskitos who reacted the most vigorously, who were displaced by the army and who participated the most in armed struggle. And it was the indigenous question which crystallized the opposition in international public opinion.

It is difficult to know the extent to which U.S. aid and the presence of the Contras played a determining role in the armed opposition of the Miskitos, or the extent to which the armed insurrection and international opinion forced Managua to alter its policy. It nevertheless remains that the Sandinista government changed direction and acknowledged some of its errors.

Three factors weighed over the negotiations and led to the compromise solution represented by the Autonomy Statutes. These were the aspirations of the Atlantic Coast peoples for sovereignty and recognition, the will of the Sandinista government not to threaten either the Republic's territorial integrity or the sharing of resources and, finally, the profound general desire for peace. Little by little, as the war abated, political negotiations took the lead. Autonomy still has to be constructed, but its principle is legally recognized. For the peoples of the Atlantic Coast, this undeniably is a step forward.

The Autonomy Statutes and the Nicaraguan Constitution

The 1987 Constitution affirmed the multiethnic character of Nicaragua and enshrined the autonomy of the Atlantic Coast as a way for its communities to exercise their rights.

The Atlantic Coast's autonomy was the object of wide-ranging debate and consultation in the communities from about 1985 on. It was legally recognized when the principle was entrenched in the new Constitution of January 1987. Articles 6, 11, 89, 90, 91, 121, 180 and 181 recognize it as one of Nicaragua's sources of wealth and list the respective rights and duties of the Atlantic Coast and the central government.[10] What are these rights?

The Constitution recognizes the multiethnic character of Nicaragua and therefore its differences (Article 6). At the same time it declares that the Atlantic Coast communities are an inseparable part of the Nicaraguan people, sharing the same obligations and enjoying the same rights as others (Article 89).

However, the communities also have their own specific rights: the right to develop their cultural identity and administer their local affairs in accordance with their own traditions and the right to preserve their traditional forms of communal land tenure and usage (Article 89). Their languages are recognized for official use within their territory and education must be provided in their mother tongue (Article 121). The State has the responsibility to guarantee them the enjoyment of their natural resources, respect for their forms of community property and free election of their authorities and representatives (Article 180). Finally, Article 181 provided that the State would adopt a law to define the system of autonomy under which the Atlantic Coast communities would exercise their rights.

The Autonomy Statutes

Law 28[11] gives official form to this autonomy, as provided in Article 181 of the Constitution. Ratified in autumn 1987, Law 28 is entitled *Autonomy Statutes of the Atlantic Coast Regions of Nicaragua*. It lays down the guiding principles for the establishment of autonomous regions and the powers of the governments which administer them.

It begins with an eight-point preamble establishing the basis of autonomy. The first point affirms the importance of transforming the political, economic and cultural order to put an end to the impoverishment, marginalization, assimilation, exploitation and extermination of the indigenous peoples of Latin America and other regions in the world.

The second point establishes the number and composition of Atlantic Coast peoples. Thus, according to the Statutes, Spanish-speaking Mestizos make up the majority (182,000), while there are 75,000 Miskitos, 26,000 Creoles, 9,000 Sumus, 1,700 Garifunas and 800 Ramas.

The fifth point declares that the process of autonomy and the recognition of Nicaragua's multiethnicity enrich the national culture and strengthen unity. This unity must be constructed from the diversity of the communities and respect for their right to preserve their identity.

The sixth point affirms that ethnic and social demands must be made simultaneously. The seventh declares that, thanks to autonomy, the communities will be able to exercise their right to share in the benefits derived from exploitation of natural resources. The communities thus must be able to create a material base that will guarantee the survival and development of their cultures.

The eighth point reaffirms that the constitutional order establishes the multiethnic character of the Nicaraguan people. It recognizes the right of communities to preserve their languages, religions, art forms and cultures, to enjoy waters, forests and communal lands and to benefit from special programs fostering their development and guaranteeing that they can organize themselves according to forms which correspond to their legitimate traditions. In fact, the Constitution recognizes special rights for the Atlantic Coast, while affirming Nicaragua's unity and territorial integrity.

It must be noted that autonomy is not recognized for the indigenous peoples themselves but for two regions, the Northern Atlantic Autonomous Region, where the indigenous people are concentrated, and the Southern Atlantic Autonomous Region, where Black Creoles are found (Article 6). Together, the two regions represent over half the Republic's territory, but less than 10 percent of the population.

The main elements of the Autonomy Statutes

The law is divided into six parts and includes 45 articles. The first part deals with the fundamental principles underlying the regions' powers.[12] The second deals with regional administrative structures, the third with revenues, the fourth with property and the fifth with the reform process. The last part contains the final and transitional provisions.

Autonomy is built around the existence of several ethnic communities on the Atlantic Coast. Consequently, Nicaragua is not a homogeneous nation but pluralistic. It must respect this character, considered to be a source of national wealth, and allow differences to flourish in harmony. To accomplish this, the Atlantic Coast needs special structures.

Dividing the Atlantic Coast into two autonomous regions allows the indigenous peoples to constitute about half the population of the Northern region (40 percent Miskitos, 8 percent Sumus, 10 percent Creoles and 40 percent Mestizos[13]) and the Creoles to assert themselves as an important minority in the Southern region. The regions' political structures reflect the multiethnic approach. Thus, each of the two regional councils and their executive organ must ensure representation of each of the region's ethnic groups.

Though multiethnic and regional, autonomy nevertheless does not recognize any inherent rights for indigenous peoples. In this regard, the terms used are totally different from those of Canadian constitutional language. Care was taken in the Statutes to never use the term "people" to designate the individuals living on the Atlantic Coast. The Statutes always refer to communities. It is the communities that own the communal lands and that define who is or is not part of the community (Article 12). The term "community," depending on the context, designates either the village or the ethnic group as a whole. For example, when reference is made to the languages of communities which will be in official use and will be taught in the schools (education in the mother tongue in the first cycle of primary school and bilingual thereafter), Miskito, Creole English, Sumu and Rama are mentioned: these clearly are larger collectivities than the village of Sandy Bay or Waspam.

Similarly, when the Statutes speak of respect for cultural identity and traditional forms of social organization and production, including collective forms of ownership and transmission, they are still referring to the rights of the inhabitants of the Atlantic Coast communities (Article 11). This ambiguity undoubtedly will give rise to much debate.

The land question, always crucial in indigenous demands, was raised throughout the autonomy discussions. In the final analysis, the Statutes make no mention of any lands purely recognized as the ancestral territory of the indigenous peoples.

The boundaries of the regions and thus the territory under their authority are established in Article 6. As we have said, this accounts for nearly half of Nicaragua's territory. The system of ownership within the regional borders is no different from the one in force in the rest of the country, except in the case of communal lands.

These are governed by Article 36, which reads as follows:

> Communal property is constituted by the lands, waters and forests which traditionally have belonged to the communities of the Atlantic Coast. They are subject to the following provisions:
> 1. Communal lands are inalienable; they may not be given, sold, seized or taxed and are indefeasible.
> 2. The inhabitants of the communities have the right to cultivate plots of communal property and may benefit from the proceeds of this work. *(Unofficial translation)*

The extent of the communal lands is not specified. Some land titles were issued when the Atlantic Coast was reintegrated into the Republic. However, according to Charles Hale,[14] these titles concern reduced areas of land. In a case studied personally by Hale, the recognized land title covered a much smaller area than the community's inhabitants believed to be their communal lands.

In the case of natural resources, Article 9 specifies that benefits will be shared:

> In the rational exploitation of mining and forest resources, fisheries and other natural resources of the autonomous regions, property rights over communal lands shall be recognized. A just proportion of this use shall benefit the region's inhabitants, through agreements between the regional and central governments. *(Unofficial translation)*

The percentage of benefits accruing to each level of responsibility, as well as the sharing of jurisdictions for the development of standards and strategies for exploitation of resources, will therefore be established by negotiation. Article 23.10 stipulates that draft legislation regarding the rational exploitation and preservation of the region's natural resources must be prepared by the Regional Council.

Autonomy in a unitary State

Unlike Canada, Nicaragua is not a federation. Its autonomous regions do not have powers equivalent to those of Canadian provinces. Instead, the regions' powers are more a matter of latitude in the application of national policies rather than real powers, like those of Québec in education, for example.

However, the regions participate in the development, planning, implementation and follow-up of the policies which concern them. The Regional Councils prepare draft legislation which is then adopted or rejected by the National Assembly. They have to lobby the delegates of the different Ministries operating on the Atlantic Coast (Article 23).

However, except in cases which purely pertain to local management, the Councils' initiatives must be ratified by the central government. Article 24 specifies that the ordinances issued by the Councils must be "in harmony" with the Constitution and laws of the Republic. This specification confers a subordinate role upon the regional governments.

With regard to revenues, taxation powers are negotiated with the central government. The regions have access to revenues from the country's general budget, as well as to a special development fund (Article 33) from autonomous revenues which are not part of the general budget. If this fund became substantial, it could provide the regions with some interesting latitude.

The Atlantic Coast Autonomy Statutes therefore do not constitute recognition of an inherent right of the First Nations, nor to an ancestral indigenous territory or an indigenous government within the meaning generally understood in Canada. Without creating such a government in the strict sense, they nevertheless recognize that the Nicaraguan nation is not ethnically homogeneous and that diversity is a source of wealth.

The Autonomy Statutes derive from a regional and multiethnic approach which allows the different groups to be represented, even if their demographic weight is small. Electoral boundaries have been redrawn for this purpose. The geographical division into two regions allows the indigenous people to constitute nearly half the voters in a territory which covers one quarter of Nicaragua. This same division also obliges them to share power and the administration with other cultures and other ways of life and to create and consolidate a multiethnic identity.

Only a small part of regional government revenues will be autonomous, but these governments essentially will have to rely on agreements to be concluded with the central government. The Statutes nevertheless clearly state the principle of revenue sharing from the exploitation of regional natural resources.

A special legal system applies to community lands, since they are inalienable and the benefits of their use go to those who work them.

The communities' languages are in official use and children, in principle, are guaranteed that they can start school in their mother tongue with curricula adopted to their reality and customs. Education will be bilingual, since Spanish also will gradually be taught. In local disputes, legal traditions will be respected. There will also be respect for social organization and modes of property transmission, to the extent that they do not contradict the Nicaraguan Constitution.

Finally, it will be up to the communities to define the criteria of their members' identity.

The Nicaraguan State does not share its sovereignty with the peoples of the Atlantic Coast and remains a unitary State. However, the creation of regional governments endowed with their own powers and revenues gives some latitude to win respect and develop a different identity. Certain ambiguities, such as those relating to the notions of community and communal land and the dual responsibility of the regions and Managua for natural resources, nonetheless, are potential sources of conflict and subject to interpretation.

The Difficult Application of the Autonomy Statutes

A product of the consultations and negotiations conducted by the Sandinista government, autonomy is being implemented with difficulty under the new government, in a region devastated by war and by an unprecedented economic crisis.

Although the Autonomy Statutes were adopted in 1987, the Atlantic Coast had to wait until May 1990 to have a regional government. This is because the regional elections scheduled for the first half of 1989 had to be postponed due to Hurricane Jane which devastated the Coast in October 1988. They finally were held at the same time as the general elections which brought Violetta Chamorro to power, confirming the special status of the Northern Atlantic Autonomous Region.

Thus, *Yatama*, the political party which won the most seats on the Regional Council (22 members and 1 deputy) is specific to the Coast and to the indigenous peoples. *Yatama* is an alliance between various Miskito nationalist tendencies (that of Brooklyn Rivera, that of Steadman Fagoth and that of the commanders who negotiated the ceasefires with the Sandinistas). *Yatama* swept most of the indigenous vote, leaving the Sandinistas only 10 to 20 percent.[15] The Sandinista wins (21 members and 1 deputy) were mainly concentrated in the mining region and among the Mestizo population. This ethnic and political cleavage marked the beginnings of the regional government and created many conflicts, particularly at the municipal level. However, this split seems to be fading away in favour of another rift between the central government and the regional governments.[16]

The delay in setting up the Regional Council allowed time for the war to end and for the refugees to return home. However, the new government had on its hands a region devastated by war, without an economic infrastructure and with several thousand former refugees still incapable of participating in production. To this immense challenge was added a lack of revenues, the lack of training of the new representatives and the absence of clear regulations for the sharing of responsibilities and for the functioning of the new structures.

Since the ratification of the Autonomy Statutes, imprecisions or ambiguities are gradually emerging. They are explained in part by the difference between the Northern and Southern regions and the central government's desire to adopt a single legislative framework. These imprecisions should have been clarified by subsequent regulation, but five years later, no regulations had been adopted!

Though several groups or institutions did submit draft regulations, no official rules have yet determined the conditions for the different levels of government to work together, nor for a clear distribution of responsibilities. Overlapping jurisdictions and conflicts easily arise in this situation.

An ambiguous role for INDERA

Once elected, President Chamorro appointed Brooklyn Rivera, a leader of *Yatama*, to head the new Atlantic Region Development Institute (INDERA). With Cabinet rank, Rivera was put in charge of co-ordinating government actions on the Coast. Although Rivera was a popular leader and a well-known autonomist, his appointment by Managua did not win unanimous support, since INDERA came under the central government rather than the regional governments. The two Regional Councils vigorously criticized the creation of the Institute, which had a larger budget than either of them. They saw this as an attempt to centralize decision-making in Managua and get around the autonomous institutions in order to deal directly with the communities. Some Sandinistas even likened INDERA to an Indian Affairs Bureau, which would be contrary to the spirit of the Autonomy Statutes. Rivera himself maintained that the Institute was an administrative agency which therefore had no conflict with the regional governments. Rivera's appointment nevertheless seems to have contributed to creating a split within *Yatama*, which was barely in control of the Northern Regional Council.

The creation of INDERA only added to the confusion surrounding the division of responsibilities. The personality conflict between Rivera and Steadman Fagoth, another *Yatama* leader with responsibilities in the regional government, poisoned relations which were already difficult.

A difficult apprenticeship in autonomy

Since the establishment of the Regional Councils in May 1990, the problem of revenues has been posed dramatically, along with that of the lack of preparation of councillors. The central government took its time allocating funds. At some points, the Regional Council could not even meet due to a lack of money. No satisfactory auditing procedures were established, with the result that the two regional co-ordinators (Aylwin Guthrie in the South and Leonel Pantin in the North) resigned from their posts with corruption charges hanging over their heads.

To add to these problems, the return of the refugees and the elimination of civil service jobs caused unemployment to soar to breathtaking heights (as high as 90 percent in Puerto Cabezas). Weak economic activity generated almost no revenues and there were not enough funds to organize a basic infrastructure.

The question of natural resources

The Northern Atlantic Region is coveted for its abundant natural resources. Its large tracts of land and its forest, mineral and marine resources are likely to attract investment. However, the short history of autonomy shows how much work remains to be done before coherent and rigourous standards are applied. Indeed, the division of jurisdictions and the protocols for negotiations are still unclear in legal terms.

On the one hand, Article 102 of the Constitution states that natural resources are a national heritage and that *it is the duty of the State to preserve the environment and ensure rational development of resources. The State may* award contracts to exploit these resources rationally when the national interest demands it.

On the other hand, the Autonomy Statutes provide that the regions "shall participate in the preparation and execution of development plans and programs" and that the Councils shall draft legislation on resource management. In addition, Article 9 specifies that "in the rational exploitation of mineral and forest resources, fisheries and other natural resources of the autonomous regions, property rights over communal lands shall be recognized. A just proportion of this use shall benefit the region's inhabitants, by means of agreements to be concluded between the regional and central governments."

At first glance, the real power over natural resources seems to rest with Managua; it nevertheless remains that the participation of regional governments in the preparation of standards for resource use and the distribution of benefits is also clearly stipulated. This means that consultation and negotiation procedures must be created. A specific case illustrates the type of problems created by the absence of such mechanisms. Equipo de Nicaragua, a Taiwanese forest company, signed a declaration of intent with the central government to operate a 375,000 hectare forestry concession in exchange for tax exemptions. But the authorities and the company negotiated without even informing the regional co-ordinator. Having learned of the matter, the Regional Council issued an order on October 12, 1991, stating that it would not allow "any concession to exploit natural resources without prior discussion and without the Council's approval." After various pressures, the project was abandoned.

In an article published in June 1992, Romero Rainero and Myrna Cunningham[17] mentioned that the Northern region had already prepared its draft legislation on management of natural resources. However, the proposed consultation procedures do not seem to have been ratified by the central government.

According to Rainero and Cunningham, any regional policy should include five major guidelines: 1) expansion of communal lands which are insufficient for the current needs of certain communities; 2) joint preparation of environmental standards applied by all; 3) policies for educating and training the people; 4) the principle of corporate reinvestment in biological, social and cultural reproduction; 5) the dual role of the Regional Councils in regulating the exploitation of resources and preparing an investment and participation policy for companies operating on the Coast. Finally, Rainero and Cunningham believe that the agreements between the communities and companies on exploitation of community resources must recognize the specific exchange traditions of these communities and the principle of compensating communities for the exploitation of their resources.

In fact, many issues are at stake concerning natural resources: the division of jurisdictions between Managua and Puerto Cabezas (who decides the standards? who chooses the companies that will exploit the resources? how will decisions be made?); the sharing of wealth generated by the exploitation of natural resources; the possibility for indigenous peoples to enforce and ensure respect for their ways of using resources (technology, relationship with the territory, etc.).

Autonomy put to the test

The effects of the war will take a long time to fade in the Northern Atlantic Region. Yet it is with this terrible heritage of a devastated territory and exacerbated conflicts that the new Regional Council must reckon. It also must deal with a central government which did not conceive the autonomy formula for the Coast and which instead tends to follow the long centralizing tradition of the Republic. Without financial resources, without solid government support, autonomy is hard to implement. The fragile gains of bilingual education are threatened. The desperate economic situation[18] increases the temptation to sell off natural wealth to the first investor who comes along, no matter what the conditions. The initial effort required to break in new structures, set up committees and parliamentary procedures and establish codes of ethics and control over elected officials is made extremely difficult by the lack of financial resources. Everything has to be done at the same time. This may partially explain the slowness with which autonomy is becoming a reality. For Myrna Cunningham, this slowness is risky:

> What the central government is trying to do is show that autonomy is not a solution. This is why it is not providing any resources and boycotting all decisions of the autonomous government. It's as if it is squandering autonomy. If things go on like this, I foresee that people will not go out to vote for autonomy in the next elections. In fact, we only have one year to prove that the autonomous government can do something.[19]

A consensus exists on three essential points, however: the current Statutes are a good starting point to meet the Coast's historical demands; regulations must be adopted to apply the Statutes; and priority must be given to creation of an economic base capable of bettering the people's living conditions.

Important gains nonetheless

The history of Nicaragua's Atlantic Coast was forged, until the end of the last century, by the Miskito-British alliance to resist first the Spaniards and then the central government. This is an essential factor in understanding the current situation. The peoples of the Coast, especially the Miskitos, are strongly influenced by this difference and their long exercise of sovereignty. Their opposition to Managua's attempts at integration came primarily from this history and their conviction that they have a distinct society.

The recognition of diversity as a source of wealth for the Nicaraguan nation has been an arduous process, since Managua's centralizing tradition had to be deconstructed. The Autonomy Statutes adopted in 1987 are considered by the peoples of the Coast to be a first step in this direction.

However, the new autonomy does not give the indigenous populations the status of a people. Instead it recognizes instead collective rights to their differences and to their protection and integration into political institutions. Autonomy, therefore, means the abandonment of attempts at assimilation.

In certain respects, the Autonomy Statutes confirm rights which have not yet been gained by the First Nations in Canada. Thus, communities themselves establish the identity of their members (not the Indian Act) and there is no Ministry of Indian Affairs in Nicaragua. INDERA, put in charge of the Coast's affairs by the central government, is headed by a Miskito. If INDERA's existence poses problems for several regional elected officials, it is that they see it as part of a centralizing trend rather than as the manifestation of ethnic subordination.

Autonomy also gives indigenous languages and Creole English official status within the territory where they are spoken, as well as the right to bilingual education. Ancestral legal traditions are recognized in the settlement of local disputes. Communal lands have a special collective ownership status. They are inalienable and subject to the traditions of the communities responsible for them. The rest of the territory of the autonomous regions is governed by national rules of property but is under the regions' jurisdiction within the limits of the powers conferred upon them.

Important ambiguities in the definition of the term "community," omnipresent in the legislative and constitutional text, give rise to conflicting interpretations. The notion of "communal lands" also risks posing the same problem. Finally, the distribution of benefits generated by exploitation of natural resources should have been stated clearly in the Statutes. What still has to be determined is the percentage (and control) of revenues which will have to be reinvested in the communities or in the region.

The multiethnic and regional approach of autonomy does not yet arouse the enthusiastic adherence of those who define themselves as nations with an ancestral territory. Thus, even though the indigenous population from now on is assured of a significant political voice, it still has to act and define itself as a multiethnic collectivity. The challenge, according to Hale, is precisely to find elements in local traditions and concerns which can fuel interest in the cause of multiethnicity and the new regional democracy. Recent history, marked by political rifts and polarization, makes it even more difficult to develop cohesion, which is nevertheless essential to the achievement of autonomy.

Lacking this cohesion, there will be neither participation by communities in regional structures, nor any possibility of efficient mechanisms for oversight and responsibility. The forced resignation of the two regional co-ordinators, accused of corruption, illustrates the problem of the lack of oversight and seriously undermines the Coast governments' ability to act.

The application of the Autonomy Statutes is also hindered by the terrible economic situation, the absence of production infrastructures and the difficulty in obtaining adequate funding from Managua. Yet relieving the misery of the people of the Atlantic Coast has become an absolute priority. Succeeding in this task is like running an obstacle course in which everything must be developed at the same time: the economic base, political responsibility, regulation, the code of ethics, etc.

In this context, there is a great risk that Managua will centralize everything and that natural resources will be exploited by parties other than the Coast communities. In this case, the people would fall back into their isolation and onto the subsistence economy by which they have survived, if barely, for so long.[20]

Nevertheless, there are three signs which give reason to believe that cohesion is slowly developing: the unified reaction of the regional governments to the creation of INDERA; the categorical refusal of the contract negotiated by Managua with the Taiwanese company, Equipo de Nicaragua; and the conciliatory attitude of some of the Coast's political representatives. The Miskito Sandinista deputy, Myrna Cunningham, gives her impressions in the following terms:

> We will have elections in 1994 and, as a Sandinista, I believe that we should not go to the polls divided. We should go there together, in alliance with other Atlantic Coast groups, with *Yatama* members who have struggled for the autonomy process, and with other political groups in the region. This is a place where it is awkward to cause polarization. We must pay attention to the way we work. In the past two years, we have managed to come together. We have succeeded in decreasing the polarization between indigenous people and non-in-

digenous people, between Sandinistas and non-San-
dinistas. The events of 1994 should not move us backward. In practical terms, we must continue to build this
Atlantic Coast with the people who defend it. In short,
we will support anyone in the government who can
protect natural resources, begin to create our economic
base and solve the problems of education and health.

The discussion and adoption of the Autonomy Statutes allowed
the debate to leave the military scene and move onto the political
stage. People now have to meet the challenge of building this
autonomy.[21]

Eyewitness Account: A Saskatchewan Cree in the Land of the Miskitos

by Marlene Larocque[22]

The time I spent on the Atlantic Coast of Nicaragua continues to hold
a special place in my heart as I was once again with the friends I met
at the *Encuentro*. It is important for them to receive visitors from other
countries, especially indigenous people, so we can experience and exchange realities. I was immediately made to feel at home, and people
were very receptive to my visit. It took some convincing to make them
believe I am indigenous, but that aspect only deepened the bonds I
developed with the people I met.

Upon arriving in Puerto Cabezas, I was immediately struck by
the difference in the environment, not just physically, but in terms of
identity and spiritual connection with the place. You leave behind the
Nicaragua that is associated with images of Managua, Leon or even
Masaya. This stems from the very different colonization processes,
one by the Spanish and the other by the British.

There is a greater level of material poverty and it hits you in the
face at every turn. The lack of infrastructure is so visible that it makes
one wonder how people survive in this situation. There exists at the
same time an incredible spirit that is exuded by the people, and it
makes one question the need for such luxuries as paved streets and
electricity 24 hours a day. (There is no structure in place to provide

round the clock electrical service during the week although it is left on Saturday and Sunday night.) Of course, although people were quick to point out all the necessary infrastructural repairs and other needs of the community, I kept questioning what effect it would have on the place. I am certain that it would mean an improvement in terms of health and standard of living, but in terms of quality of life would it significantly improve anything?

Then came the big debate about autonomy. These people love to talk about the subject and can tell you how they would have done it and what changes they would implement, given the chance. Since I spent a lot of time with women and youth, it was especially good to get that perspective that is so often ignored by official structures.

The general feeling I got about the autonomy deal was that it was good in principle and concept but something went wrong when it came time to put it into practice. Of course, all deals usually suffer in the transition from paper to community reality, and it takes great political courage on the part of leaders to ensure a smooth transition. The youth I spoke with are still young and were not at the negotiating table, but speak highly of their elders and elected officials. The women continue to feel isolated from the whole process.

The Autonomy package established the creation of two regional governments, one each in Bluefields and Puerto Cabezas. As the country grapples with structural adjustment policies of funding agencies, fewer resources are available and the poorest sectors of society are the most affected. The two regional governments are receiving barely enough funds for the operating costs of their offices, but no real funding for social, health or housing programs.

At the same time, the gap between wealthy and poor continues to widen. You can see some families and individuals who are well off. They live in nicer housing, drive fancy trucks and live in Managua. Alongside this reality, there exist people who have nothing but one another. In this situation you find examples of true solidarity because that is the only way to survive. This is an example of an alternative economy.

The Atlantic Coast is rich with natural resources which have been extracted by foreigners and have created wealth for faraway places with no real investment in the region. Ports and roads were built for the sole purpose of moving lumber, gold and lobsters out of the region, not for the benefit of the local people. This is a reflection of the process over the past 500 years when examining the situation of indigenous peoples in the Americas. We can see the exact same reality in northern Saskatchewan, and this trend continues. The true costs of these developments have been suffered by the indigenous people as the erosion of the environment coincides with the erosion of human rights and lack of control over land and resources.

The national government in Managua continues to look to the Coast as a place where natural resources can be exploited and sold to foreigners in their search for revenue in the midst of the worst economic crisis to hit the country. The Atlantic Coast receives all its food, clothing, medicines and household necessities from Managua. This leaves the people of the Coast with few options in terms of economic development strategies, so when opportunities arise to generate needed revenues, they usually accept what is offered. The lack of any real manufacturing base which would bring not only jobs , but sustainable development is an important preoccupation of the people.

Unfortunately, the autonomy process has received enormous attention, making it the one issue that is being dealt with. At the same time, there has been a decrease in health, social and living standards that have not received as much attention. By focusing on one aspect of the needs of the people, the gap between the leaders and the grassroots has widened. While men like Brooklyn Rivera and Steadman Fagoth continue to wage a war of words and seek political attention, people are struggling to make ends meet.

It is still unclear to the people how autonomy translates into their everyday lives and whether it will improve anything. As with all indigenous communities, there seems to be an elite created with these processes of establishing new governments. Many leaders have been seen as selling out to the governments while breaking their ties to the traditional authorities in the face of pressure to conform to the larger national agenda.

Notes

1.   Eleonore Von OErtzen, *El colonialismo britanico y el reino Misquito en los siglos XVII y XVIII, Encuentro,* nos 24-25, April to September 1985, pp. 5-28.
2.   Von OErtzen, op. cit., p. 8.
3.   Charles Hale, "Inter-Ethnic Relations and Class Structures in Nicaragua's Atlantic Coast: An Historical Overview," in CIDCA and Development Study Unit, *Ethnic Groups and the Nation State, The Case of the Atlantic Coast in Nicaragua,* Stockholm, University of Stockholm, 1987, pp. 33-57.

4. Charles Hale, op. cit., and CAPRI, *Region Autonoma del Atlantica Norte, El desafio de la Autonomia*, Centro Humbolt, 1992.

5. The Moravian Church is a religious group derived from the Hussite sect (1457).

6. Jorge Jenkins Molieri. *El desafio indigena en Nicaragua. El caso de los Miskitos*. Ed. Vanguardia, 1986.

7. Linda Rossbach and Winderich Volker, "Derechos indigenas y estado nacional en Nicaragua. La convencion Misquita de 1894." *Encuentro* 24-25, 1985, pp. 29-54.

8. *Mestizo* is the term used to designate colonists originating from the Pacific Coast. See Appendix II: "The peoples of Nicaragua's Atlantic Coast."

9. CAPRI, 1992, op. cit.

10. Constitucion Politica de Nicaragua, Ed. El Amenecer, February 1987.

11. Republica de Nicaragua, "Estatuto de la Autonomia de las Regiones de la Costa Atlantica de Nicaragua," ley no 28, *La Gaceta*, Diario oficial, October 30, 1987.

12. See Appendix III: "The fundamental principles of the Autonomy Statutes ...."

13. CAPRI, op. cit., p. 108.

14. Charles Hale, "Wan tasbaya dukiara, Nociones contenciosas de los derechos sobre la tierra en la Historia Miskita," *Wani*, Revista des Caribe nicaraguense, CIDCA-UCA, no 12, July 1992, pp. 1-19.

15. Charles R. Hale, "Miskitu. Revolution in the Revolution," *Report on the Americas, the First Nations*, NACLA, vol. XXV, no 3, Dec. 1991.

16. CAPRI, *Region Autonoma del Atlantica Norte, El desafio de la Autonomia*, Centro Humbolt, 1992.

17. Romero Rainero and Myrna Cunningham, "Autonomia y recursos naturales," *Wani*, Revista del Caribe nicaraguense, CIDCA-UCA, no 12, July 1992, pp. 48-58.

18. See Appendix IV: "General Data and Living Conditions in the Northern Atlantic Autonomous Region."

19. Interview with Myrna Cunningham, Sandinista deputy from the Atlantic Coast, October 1992. In the 1994 elections, 44,524 of the 59,789 registered voters voted. 15,000 abstained.

20. Pierre Beaucage, "Gens de la pirogue et du bananier: la mobilité spatiale chez les Miskitos," *Recherches amérindiennes au Québec*, vol. XXIII, no 4, 1993, pp. 39-61.

21. The 1994 elections considerably altered the political landscape of the NAAR. The Constitutional Liberal Party (PLC), described as Somozist, won 19 seats, tied with the Sandinista Front (19). *Yatama*, some of whose leaders had switched to the PLC (Steadman Fagoth), only obtained 7 seats.

22. Marlene Larocque is a political science student. A Saskatchewan Cree, she is a member of the Jeanne Sauvé Foundation for Young Leaders. She made a trip to Central America in 1992 on behalf of CUSO, the Canadian Union of Students Overseas, an international co-operation agency.

Chapter 3

Colombia: A Multiethnic and Pluricultural Society

by The National Organization of Indigenous Peoples of Colombia (ONIC)[1]

Participation of Colombian Indigenous Peoples in the Constitutional Reform of 1991

by the ONIC team at the Constituent Assembly

In the past few years, it had become urgent to overhaul the Colombian Constitution. The political model based on the two traditional parties had engendered exclusion and maintained the country in a permanent state of siege for 30 years. It was a crisis. Never had Congress been so discredited. Social forces were struggling to be heard. Redoubled violence degenerated into massacres every second day. Peace talks initiated with the guerrilla groups were leading nowhere. During two electoral periods, four candidates for the Presidency of the Republic had been murdered. Ethnic and religious tensions were surfacing. The war on the drug trade had turned to terrorism. In short, the country could no longer continue with the institutions inherited from the Colombia of 1886.

The struggle for access to the Assembly

The process leading to the new Constitution began in 1988, when the government decided to resort to a plebiscite. However, the State Council opposed this, considering it contrary to the Constitution. Students then fought for the formation of a National Constituent Assembly by calling directly on the people to convene one. The proposal aroused a favourable response, and the people convened the Assembly in elections held on December 1, 1990. However, half the potential electorate abstained from voting.

ONIC got involved in the process from the start, aware that the time was right to make the dynamic presence of 82 indigenous peoples felt in the country, to entrench in the Constitution all of the rights demanded by the indigenous movement during 20 years of struggle and thus put an end to 500 years of invisibility and outrage. "We have come out of oblivion to kindle new hopes," ONIC said in its message to the Colombian people.

The indigenous peoples of Colombia, therefore, participated actively in the working groups which were organized everywhere in Colombia, even in the most remote regions, from 1988 to 1990. ONIC also participated in all meetings bringing together the different social organizations interested in the constitutional reform. However, it was the IIIrd National Indigenous Congress which gave ONIC the most visibility. This meeting assembled nearly 5000 indigenous people in Bosa in June 1990.

The IIIrd Congress defined the main lines of the constitutional proposal, which consisted of two parts: proposals of national interest (democracy, human rights, ecology, public force) and specifically indigenous proposals (multiethnicity, ethnic groups, territorial autonomy, cultural identity, collective ownership of the land).

The IIIrd Congress also designated Francisco Rojas Birry of the Embera ethnic group (Pacific Basin tropical forest) as the ONIC candidate to the Constituent Assembly. It must be said that the various social organizations had to exert pressure to obtain access to the Assembly. However, neither the government nor the four political parties which had participated in the decisions concerning its preparation had access to the Assembly. This is why the indigenous peoples were able to participate in the elections on the same terms as the other candidates.

It is worth noting that ONIC had no electoral experience. It was unfamiliar with both electoral legislation and the tricks of the trade, well known to experienced candidates. In fact, until then ONIC had shared the abstentionist policy of the Left, even though it respected the will of its grassroots members to participate in elections. Electoralism simply was not part of ONIC's agenda. Its greatest weakness was its limited electorate. Not only was this the first time that ONIC was participating in elections, but its specifically indigenous social base was extremely small (barely 2 percent of the population, the majority of whom had no identification card and lived far from the polling stations).

Our only advantage came from the fact that, for this election, the 70 delegates to the Constituent Assembly would be elected from a national electoral district. It would thus be possible to vote for a candidate regardless of one's place of residence in Colombia. And for the first time, a large piece of cardboard showing the candidates' photos replaced the usual ballots. These two measures put an end to the proverbial manipulative power of the traditional political bosses and provincial power brokers. Also playing in our favour was the solidarity created by the rejection of the celebrations marking the 500th anniversary of the European invasion.

Our *compañero*'s election campaign held the full attention of ONIC's 34 regional, zone and local organizations. It invested all its resources in the campaign. However, ONIC's first objective was to mobilize ideas, since the aboriginal movement had to develop a mentality and discourse not limited solely to indigenous peoples and therefore capable of encompassing the entire nation, arousing the interest of the non-indigenous majority of Colombians whose votes were absolutely necessary to us. Fortunately, this path was familiar to us. Since the beginning of the indigenous struggles in the late 1960s and early 1970s, we had always worked side by side with popular groups and our struggles had been part of the national context. Thus, our demands were identical to those of other excluded and mistreated groups. Moreover, we were convinced that we had something new to say to a tired country and that we could make a great contribution to the search for a way out of the crisis, thanks to such questions as: Who are we for as Colombians? Where do we come from? What are our elementary realities (ethnic, human, territorial)? This is why we adopted another slogan which was widely accepted: "From our roots and for our dreams, for everyone."

Finally, thanks to the massive support of regions with concentrated indigenous populations and the votes of many Colombian men and women, our *companero*, Francisco Rojas Birry, was elected to the Constituent Assembly on December 1, 1990. Another *compañero*, Lorenzo Muelas Hurtado, of the regional movement Southwestern Indigenous Authorities (AISO), was also elected. AISO became known throughout the country during these elections, having received the support of the voters.

On this historic December 1, the people elected 70 delegates. Later, after agreements concluded with the government, four representatives of demobilized guerrilla groups entered the Constituent

Assembly, including a third indigenous *compañero*, Alfonso Pena Chepe, of the Quintin Lame Indigenous Movement.

An organized indigenous participation

Once *compañero* Rojas Birry was elected to the Assembly, ONIC, aware of its incumbent responsibility, hastened to organize a support group for its representative. Rojas Birry thus had his own office, a computer, some leeway to work (although he stayed in permanent contact with the Executive Committee) and four teams involving a total of 15 full-time people. The administration of the Assembly only defrayed the cost of one counsellor and two assistants per delegate. The four teams were as follows:

- The administrative team, which co-ordinated the other teams and ensured the efficient operation of the group and the secretarial, messenger and escort services, kept the office clean and made coffee;
- The political team, made up of two indigenous *companeros* from regional organizations and delegates from other ethnic groups (Blacks and Insular Natives, as the people from the San Andrés Archipelago are called), which ensured follow-up with the Constituent Assembly and maintained relations with other social groups (workers, women, teachers, environmentalists, human rights organizations, etc.);
- The communications team, made up of three journalists, who fed the media, transmitted news from the Assembly to the regional organizations and informed the other delegates of ONIC's positions. For this purpose, they edited a periodical newsletter entitled the *Indigenous Constituent*, eight issues of which were published;
- The technical team, which consisted of three lawyers specializing in indigenous legislation, public law and human rights. They took on the task of presenting the proposals defined by the IIIrd National Congress in the appropriate legal language and ensuring constant follow-up of the indigenous proposals in the Assembly's various committees.

Every morning at 7 a.m., the four teams met to plan their tasks for the day.

ONIC's proposals

From 1988 to 1991, ONIC devoted its efforts to the debate on the proposals, before confronting them with those of the government and the other groups or parties in the working groups. Areas of recognition were thus opened up and a vision of the country took shape. In November 1990, we drafted *The Colombia We Want* and succeeded in formulating a proposal integrating the country's different ethnic groups.

The Colombia We Want was the title of the constituent proposal addressed to the nation by the indigenous peoples represented by ONIC. We proposed a Colombia that would be:

- Democratic (participatory and pluralist democracy, territorial reorganization, social participation, representation of minorities);
- Respectful of human rights (right to life and dignity, social rights, elimination of all forms of discrimination, responsibility of the executive power, forms of control without resorting to state of siege or martial law, civilian police);
- Capable of guaranteeing justice and peace (ideological and political tolerance, political solutions to conflicts, people's wardens and justices of the peace);
- Protective of the environment (common heritage, rational use of natural resources, biodiversity and preservation of ecosystems, environmental land use plan, territories, education, protection of the environment, integral agrarian reform);
- Favourable to economic development (mixed economy, guarantees for the solidarity economy, participatory planning, agrarian reform, economic openness, settlement of the foreign debt).

"Land, Culture and Autonomy"

In deciding, at the IIIrd Indigenous National Congress, to participate in the Constituent Assembly, we undertook to defend and demand not only the rights of indigenous peoples but also, and in a very direct manner, those of all of the country's ethnic groups. For in addition to the interests and problems which drew us closer to them, there were common struggles, particularly for the defence of the Pacific shoreline. It was therefore out of the question for ONIC to show up at the Constituent Assembly with an exclusively indigenous position. The Organization needed an ethnic position, which had been defined in the working groups in 1988, thanks to the important contribution of researchers in anthropology, linguistics and other social sciences.

There are nearly 3 million Blacks in Colombia.[2] They live mainly on the Pacific Coast, in communities where land and culture integrate naturally. In the Atlantic, 700 kilometres from the coast, Insular Natives live on the Colombian archipelago of San Andrés and Providencia. Originating from other islands in the West Indies, they have their own language, culture and religion. We, the 800,000 indigenous people, are spread throughout Colombia in 82 different peoples, speaking 64 distinct languages. The largest indigenous population is found in the provinces of Cauca, Choco and Guajira (the indigenous population occupying the largest territory lives in the provinces of Amazonia and Orinoquia).

As indigenous peoples, Blacks and San Andrés Natives, we have always been excluded, belittled and made victims of discrimination. We have suffered the violent pillage of our territories or been forced to move by economic, social or military measures. The map of our current dwelling places overlaps the poverty map and our cultures have been persecuted and subjected to integration policies in the name of Western culture, someone's God or national sovereignty.

This is why, having been in permanent contact with Black and San Andrés Native organizations, we submitted proposals to the Constituent Assembly giving highest priority to the principle of "recognition of the multiethnic and multicultural character of the Colombian people."

This principle also appeared in the draft presented by the government to the Assembly, but only at the beginning of the paragraph entitled *The rights of indigenous peoples,* as if this principle were a right only for them, when in fact it concerns all Colombians and, for this reason, involves a fundamental change in the national identity. With this principle, the nation would cease to be unitary in the homogeneous sense (one race, one language, one culture, one authority, one religion) and henceforth would recognize its unity in diversity.

Based on the recognition of ethnic and cultural diversity, a series of practical consequences were then proposed. To this end, and without claiming to cover every group, we used the motto of the indigenous movement, "Land, Culture, Autonomy" as our guide.

The main right to be demanded for indigenous peoples, Blacks and San Andrés Natives was ownership of the land. This right is indispensable to our physical and cultural survival and to the preservation of ecosystems as fragile as those of the Sierra Nevada de Santa Marta, Amazonia, the San Andrés Archipelago, the Pacific Basin and, in general, our current habitats.

However, since our rights are interrelated, our struggle encompassed all of them. We would make no progress in recovering our territories if we did not also have the necessary autonomy to live there, the capacity of a people to define and meet its cultural, economic, political, religious and social needs. This is why it was essential that the Constitution recognize the right of our peoples to develop economically and socially, with their own authorities and preserving their identity.

This purpose was unattainable unless far-reaching decentralization was instituted, putting an end to the political centralism by which the State, over the past 100 years, has demonstrated its inability to serve our territories except with its army.

In constitutional terms, such autonomy could only be expressed by the concept of a space specific to San Andrés Natives, Blacks and indigenous peoples within the country's administrative political division. This meant considering the ethnic territories as territorial entities.

We thus made a proposal which reflected a general trend in the Constituent Assembly. The Assembly was seeking to reorganize the territory completely, since the existing disorder, while harmful to ethnic groups, was no more suitable to the majority of Colombians.

Above all, we could not allow our different cultures to die out. The origins of the indigenous peoples, Blacks and Insular Natives differ, as do our respective modes of development. Each of the three groups, under its special conditions, has preserved its own cultural characteristics which distinguish it from the rest of the Colombian population, but which at the same time enrich the culture and identities of the entire Colombian people.

Culture is manifested in our music, our religions and our myths, in our languages and education, in our medicinal and curative practices, in our diet, in our way of exercising authority and social control, in how we use the resources offered by the land.

It is therefore culture which both distinguishes and unites us in this struggle. But to preserve and reproduce our culture, we need our territory and autonomy. The two are inseparable, and we will get nowhere without them.

We also formulated proposals regarding a specific indigenous jurisdiction, dual citizenship for indigenous peoples in border regions, political representation in Congress and others. Together, we asked that these proposals be grouped in a separate chapter of the Constitution.

Functioning of the Assembly

Decision-making in the Constituent Assembly was marked by its unusual voting patterns. No political party had the absolute majority of delegates. Even if they joined together, the Liberal and Conservative parties fell short of a majority. The April 19 Movement (M-19) — born out of the demobilization of the guerrilla group of the same name — obtained a large number of delegates, as did the National Salvation Movement (MSN), a "supra-party" conservative movement. This reality obliged the Assembly to adopt a collegial presidency shared by the Liberal Party, M-19 and the MSN. In addition, the following minorities obtained two seats each: indigenous peoples, evangelicals, the Patriotic Union (a party resulting from the peace talks with the Colombian Revolutionary Armed Forces) and the Hope, Peace and Freedom Party (also resulting from the demobilization of the National Liberation Army). Two former armed groups, the Quintin Lame National Liberation and the Workers' Revolutionary Party, each obtained one seat without the right to vote.

It must be noted that two guerrilla groups, the Colombian Revolutionary Armed Forces (FARC) and the National Liberation Army (ELN), maintained their belligerent status during and after the Assembly.

The government was constantly present and participated in all of the Assembly's debates and decisions.

Organizationally, the Assembly had its own decision-making process. Five committees had been created: Principles and Rights; Territorial Organization; Congress and Government; Justice; and Economy. The committees would approve an article which went to the Plenary Assembly for first reading. The article then went to the Codification Committee and came back to the Plenary for second reading. Out of this would come the constitutional texts.

The indigenous delegates shared the work as follows: Francisco Rojas Birry participated in the Principles and Rights Committee. The first debate concerned the inclusion of the name of God in the Constitution, because of the diversity of beliefs among the indigenous peoples. The Commission approved the principle of ethnic and cultural diversity, the list of human rights, guardianship, participatory democracy, the official status of the languages of the different ethnic groups and the ownership of their communal lands and of indigenous *resguardos*.[3] Francisco Rojas Birry also covered a large part of the work of Committees III, IV and V which had no indigenous members and which approved the first texts concerning ethnic representation in Congress, indigenous jurisdiction and the budget provided for the indigenous territories.

Lorenzo Muelas and Alfonso Pena Chepe sat on Committee II, which dealt with territorial organization and, within the context of this subject, the possibilities of autonomy for the territories of the different ethnic groups.

Blacks and Insular Natives, who had no delegate to represent them, chose to engage in systematic lobbying with delegates of various tendencies.

In addition to the personal presence of indigenous Assembly members on the committees, there were visits by many indigenous delegations from everywhere in Colombia to make symbolic cultural presentations to the Assembly. For example, the Cauca Regional Indigenous Council (CRIC) symbolically presented the Paeces baton of chieftaincy to the three Assembly Presidents.

In addition to these presentations, ONIC campaigned throughout the country for an earlier plebiscite, delivering over 50,000 votes to the Assembly in favour of dissolution of the old Congress, on the same day that the Assembly decided to revoke the mandate of the members of Congress and call for the establishment of a new Congress.

The Colombian press paid special attention to the indigenous delegates, though on many occasions, because they themselves objected, it focused more on novelty and folklore than on the proposals which were submitted.

The debate on the indigenous proposals

From the start, the climate was favourable to the indigenous proposals. Several constitutional reform projects submitted by the delegates of the different parties, including the government, took up the proposals which ONIC had advanced over the past three years.

However, most of these proposals recognized cultural rights without any specific definition and proposed nothing concrete in terms of autonomy or economic resources (including the fate reserved for the natural resources of the indigenous territories). For example, the government simply proposed that the different public organizations "pay special attention" to the indigenous territories.

The proposal concerning indigenous territories, understood as territorial entities, was in tune with the majority position of the Assembly, which favoured a territorial reorganization which would include autonomy for departments and municipalities and create new administrative divisions, such as provinces and regions. The indigenous demand for territorial entities painfully illustrated that a new arrangement was necessary.

As the Assembly progressed and the delegates became aware of the country's multiethnicity and the scope of the indigenous proposals in this sense, the following main objections were raised:

- Instead of including a specific chapter on ethnic groups, the question should be dispersed through various titles of the Charter;
- Collective ownership of land would be a historic setback;
- The Black or San Andrés and Providencia Native communities could not be conceded the same rights as those recognized to indigenous peoples, because the latter had retained their cultural identity.

This debate was lively, especially when territorial rights had to be defined. To the very end, the Assembly refused to recognize Blacks as a separate ethnic group. Only at the last minute were they acknowledged the right of ownership of their ancestral lands, but not as administrative political territorial entities. The ownership rights of the Insular Natives were not even protected; the Assembly only accepted that the population of the archipelago be controlled and that this group be given the possibility of expressing itself at the municipal level.

In any case, it proved to be very significant that an integral ethnic proposal was presented, since the concept of ethnic groups, covering the three ethnic groups and remaining open to others, was acknowledged in various locations, as it was in the official status of their languages, in education and communal lands, in recognition of ethnic diversity and the equality of cultures, and in special access to the House of Representatives.

It should also be noted that ethnic groups were treated nowhere in the new Constitution as minorities, marginal people or vulnerable sectors. We were recognized for what we are: an organic component of the nation. It may happen, as in the case of other social groups, that we are victims of discrimination, marginalized or more vulnerable. This, however, will not derive from our ethnicity, but rather from the social conditions in which we live.

As for the term "indigenous peoples," which is totally rejected almost everywhere else in the world, it was readily accepted by the Assembly, perhaps because the Colombian indigenous movement has not made terminological questions the central focus of its struggles.

On the issue of ownership of natural resources, ONIC launched the debate in 1988 with the Mining Code. The new Constitution took up the same elements as the old one, despite the battle waged by delegate Alfonso Peña who again wanted to entrust the indigenous peoples with ownership of underground resources. Finally, it was recognized that natural resources in the indigenous territories could not be exploited to the detriment of the communities' ethnic integrity, but that it should depend on their participation.

The existence of indigenous jurisdiction was accepted without difficulty by Committee IV and by the Plenaries, even though it had to be imperfectly subject to the laws of the Republic.

The favourable reception given to our proposals lasted through first reading in the Constituent Assembly, which approved them by a majority. However, this initial gain ran into trouble at the Codification Committee which attempted to reject most of the points won in first reading. Rojas Birry, as a member of this Committee, expressed his disagreement and insisted that the original texts be respected. In any case, he subsequently dissociated himself from the Committee to present his own codification, which ultimately was not taken into account because of the rush of business in the final sessions.

In second reading, certain indigenous initiatives were rejected, with some of their initial supporters now voting against. This was the case for dual citizenship for indigenous peoples in border regions. At first they were granted this by right of birth, erasing the injustice committed against peoples divided by borders which had nothing to do with their own history. But subsequently, opponents said that it would be electorally risky for the Wayuus of Venezuela, the Tucanos of Brazil, the Kunas of Panama or the Awas of Ecuador to have the possibility of acceding to the Colombian Presidency.

The territorial proposal was also severely truncated in second reading. The government, which had not expressed itself on the question either in Committee II or in first reading, took a stand during second reading against indigenous territorial entities and internal government functions. The indigenous delegates then said they preferred to withdraw from the Constituent Assembly if they were only to be recognized ownership of the land (already provided in Law 89 adopted in 1890 and then defended at the price of costly struggles) without also assuring them the right to territorial autonomy. The Assembly marked time for two days because of this last-minute obstacle. Finally, on the last day of deliberations, the right to indigenous territorial entities was recognized.

The Rights of Ethnic Groups in the New Colombian Constitution

by the ONIC legal team

After an educational effort and intense negotiations among the 74 delegates and with the government, the three indigenous representatives to the Constituent Assembly managed to have the new Constitution redefine the nation in terms of multiethnicity and multiculturalism, as the basis for defining the rights of ethnic groups.

These rights can be grouped under the following headings: principles, culture, property, indigenous territories, autonomy, resources, nationality, political representation and justice.[4]

The principles

Among the fundamental principles of the Constitution is one whereby *the State shall recognize and protect the ethnic and cultural diversity of the Colombian nation* (Article 7).

This principle makes it possible to put an end to the century-old tradition of denying the real composition of the Colombian people, claiming to unify the population and culture and seeking, through government policies, to integrate ethnic groups by force or dissuasion into the culture and markets of the national society.

Further on, in the chapter on social, economic and cultural rights, a second principle appears: *The State shall recognize the equality and dignity of all cultures which live together in the country* (Article 70).

This principle of the equality of all cultures should not only end discrimination between cultures. It also will contribute greatly to resolving conflicts of application between rules of customary law and statute law.

The culture

This chapter begins with the clarification that by recognizing the multiethnic and multicultural character of the nation, the national identity is enriched and not only the specific cultural identity of ethnic groups.

The languages and dialects of these groups are declared official in their territories, along with Spanish which is the official language of Colombia. This means that education in communities with their own linguistic tradition must be bilingual.

In the same sense, members of ethnic groups are recognized to have the right to education which respects and develops their cultural identity (Article 68), meaning that research must not be pursued on indigenous languages with the aim of teaching them the Bible.

Provision is also made for special mechanisms to protect the cultural identity of Black communities (transitional Article 55) and San Andrés Natives (Article 310), as well as the cultural integrity of the indigenous peoples (Article 330).

Property

The new Constitution creates a new category of property: ownership of communal lands by ethnic groups. These lands henceforth are inalienable, indefeasible and unseizable (Article 63). The law is responsible for developing this new category, which will benefit indigenous peoples, Blacks and Natives.

The Constitution also protects the potential special rights of ethnic groups inhabiting territories containing archaeological treasures (Article 72).

In the case of Blacks, the Constitution provides for adoption of a law recognizing the right of Black communities to collective ownership of fallow land which they have occupied in zones along the rivers of the Pacific slope. According to Blacks' traditional production practices, this right cannot be alienated freely. Moreover, it may extend to similar zones elsewhere in Colombia. The government must adopt a law favouring the economic and social development of these zones in the 2 years after the Constitution comes into force. The law must designate the government itself as responsible for the performance of this mandate. The territorial boundaries must be defined with the communities' representatives (Article 55).

The care taken in identifying Black communities which will acquire this right is explained by the difficulty the delegates had, in certain cases, in agreeing to characterize the Black population as an ethnic group distinct from other Colombians.

As for Insular Natives, the Constitution did not really guarantee their ancestral rights to the lands of the archipelago. It only envisages measures intended to protect their cultural identity, the environment and natural resources. The law thus makes it possible to limit the alienation of landed property, population density and land use (Article 310). In the meantime, the government must regulate the population density of the islands (transitional Article 42).

The indigenous peoples were guaranteed collective and indefeasible ownership of the lands of their *resguardos*. This property cannot be ceded, alienated or seized (Articles 63 and 329).

Special regulations were also established for the exploitation of natural resources in the territories inhabited by indigenous peoples. However, these resources may not be exploited to the detriment of the cultural, social and economic integrity of the communities, since the government must ensure the participation of indigenous representatives in the decisions made concerning this exploitation (Article 330). It is curious that, contrary to what is being done for departments and municipalities, this system has not provided for payment of any direct royalties for indigenous territories in exchange for this exploitation (Article 360).

Indigenous territories

To various degrees, there has been territorial recognition of ownership for all ethnic groups.

But for indigenous peoples, this recognition encompasses and goes beyond the recognition provided by administrative policy. Indeed, the major debate in the Constituent Assembly concerned the territorial reorganization which would replace the traditional departments and municipalities with new entities which will take into account geographical, environmental, social, anthropological and cultural aspects.

Indigenous territories thus have been constituted as territorial entities, on the same basis as departments, districts and municipalities, with the possibility that regions and provinces will also be constituted in the future (Article 286).

This means that the indigenous territories enjoy autonomy in the management of their interests. This gives them the right to govern themselves, exercise their own jurisdictions, manage resources, levy the taxes necessary for their functions and share in national non-tax revenues (Article 287).

The indigenous peoples proposed that the new territorial entities include both the reserves and the territories traditionally occupied by indigenous peoples. The government wanted to limited them only to the reserves. Since there was no constitutional agreement, the indigenous territories will be formed under the provisions of the Organic Law on Territorial Reorganization. It will be up to the government, the representatives of the indigenous communities and the Territorial Reorganization Commission to determine the new boundaries. This law will also define the relations and co-ordination between the indigenous territories and the other units (Article 329).

To speed up the establishment of territories without it being necessary to wait for application of the law, the government was authorized to decree the fiscal and other standards necessary for the territories to function and co-ordinate with other entities (transitional Article 56).

Autonomy

The Insular Natives of the San Andrés Archipelago were not recognized to have their own autonomy in that their territories were not considered to be ethnic territorial entities. However, the total elimination of intendancies and commissionerships today gives the archipelago the status of a department. The Constitution provided that when new municipalities are created, the Departmental Assembly would guarantee the institutional expression of the native communities (Article 310).

Neither were any special provisions adopted for the Black communities of the Pacific Coast and other like communities. Nevertheless, a special mode of administration undoubtedly will have to be designed for them in order to regulate collective ownership and implement the legal mechanisms to protect their culture and promote their development.

The Constitution recognizes the reserve organization of the indigenous peoples, of which the Councils are an essential component. At the same time, they are entitled to a new form of government specific to the territorial entity status of the indigenous territories.

In indigenous territorial entities, the government will be made up of councils formed and regulated by the usages and customs of their communities and conforming to the Constitution and laws (Article 330).

However, this standard does not subject these councils to rigid rules, since it recognizes the great variety of forms of authority which exist among the indigenous peoples, such as councils, elders, *caciques*, *mamos*, clan chiefs, etc.

The Constitution does not only entrench the autonomy of the authorities of the indigenous peoples. It also entrenches their normative autonomy by raising the usages and customs of their communities to rank as sources of law.

The Councils take over the functions regarding the following questions: land use, peopling of territories, development plans and programs, public investments, fiscal resources, natural resources, programs for communities inhabiting the territories, public order and government representation.

Most of these functions are not decisional. However, they contribute to the steps of promotion, design, protection, implementation and control, thus providing the Councils with an important governmental function.

The Constitution also provides for special treatment for indigenous territories which overlap various departments before their conversion into territorial entities. In these cases, the territories are administered by indigenous Councils in co-ordination with the governments of the departments in question (Article 329).

Resources

The Constitution adopted new criteria for the distribution of resources among the territorial entities. Among these criteria, we may note the participation of municipalities in the nation's current revenues since 1993. Thus, this participation has extended to the indigenous *resguardos* determined by law, which must define the priority fields of social investment to be funded with these resources (Article 357 and transitional Article 45).

To benefit from this distribution, a *resguardo*, therefore, does not have to be transformed into a territorial entity or integrated into an indigenous territorial entity.

As territorial entities, the indigenous territories do not receive transfers of current national revenues or direct royalties from exploitation of non-renewable natural resources. However, they have their own revenue sources, such as a share of national non-tax revenues (Article 287, no 4), levying of taxes (Article 287, no 3), resources which the Councils may collect and distribute (Article 330, no 4), royalties received from ports located in the territory or the National Royalties Fund (Articles 360 and 361), debt financing (Article 295), etc.

It should also be remembered that the President of Colombia has been given the power to decree the fiscal measures necessary for the indigenous territorial entities to function (transitional Article 56).

Nationality

The indigenous peoples asked the Constituent Assembly to recognize that, before the formation of Nation-States, people lived in what are now the border areas between Latin American countries. They therefore asked that Colombian citizenship be granted, by right of birth, to members of indigenous peoples in border areas. The proposal passed first reading but underwent major changes: they were recognized as Colombian citizens, but by adoption and with application of the principle of reciprocity in accordance with public treaties (Article 96, no 2).

Even with this amendment, the proposal creates a precedent in Latin America. It is hoped that other countries will follow this example.

Political representation

All ethnic groups wanted easier access to the State institutions that their low population density and geographical dispersion had hitherto denied them. They obtained a special electoral district to elect up to five representatives to the House in order to ensure participation by ethnic groups, as did political minorities and Colombians residing out of the country (Article 176).

A special national electoral district was established for the Senate, to which the indigenous communities elect two Senators.

Justice

In addition to administrative political recognition, the authority always exercised by the indigenous peoples was now recognized.

The Constitution provides that the authorities of the indigenous peoples can exercise jurisdiction over their territories according to their own standards and procedures, on the condition that they do not oppose the Constitution or the laws of the Republic (Article 246).

The indigenous authorities therefore have been given general authorization to administer justice in their respective territories, in broader terms than their usages and customs and in accordance with their own standards and procedures. This gives them great normative capacity to make up for the deficiencies of the current system.

The law will establish how to bring this special jurisdiction into line with the national judicial system.

Final comments

Far from being a set of more or less kindhearted concessions to the indigenous peoples and other ethnic groups, the ethnic rights henceforth included in the Constitution are the outcome of a long struggle for unity, land, autonomy and culture, in the image of ONIC's guiding principles and the ancestral resistance of the Black and San Andrés Native peoples to the process of despoilment and acculturation.

These rights also correspond to the emergence of a new awareness in Colombian society which could not have seen the light of day under the exclusive and unitary canons of the 1886 Constitution. This constitutional recognition of ethnic diversity also depends, no doubt, on the necessity for the government to endow obsolete institutions, out of tune with the times, with new legitimacy.

With these new rights a twofold transformation begins, emanating from the indigenous communities and other ethnic groups to national society as a whole, and vice versa. The traditional conception of ethnic groups has changed, and so have government policies.

Two Years Later: A Critical Look at the Achievements of the New Constitution

by the ONIC Central Bureau

July 5, 1993 marked the second anniversary of the enactment of the new Constitution.

We, as indigenous people, all know that we were fully involved in the convening and deliberations of the Constituent Assembly. Our participation dates from the IIIrd National Congress which was held in Bosa in 1990. At that time, we defined our participation as another step in our traditional struggles. This is confirmed by the conclusions of the IIIrd Congress, which included the following statement:

> What we will win in the new Constitution and what we will succeed in obtaining in practice will depend on the strength of our struggle, based on unity. This having been said, the victories that we will obtain at the Constituent Assembly *do not represent the final objective of our struggle. Rather, they are a means to move on to new gains.*

Today we find that issues related to the new Constitution are taking up a large part of our energy and much of the human and financial resources at our disposal. Therefore, within the framework of this new exceptional National Indigenous Congress, which is being held three years after the last, it will be worth the effort to engage in critical analysis of the new Constitution's influence on our organizations, on the life of indigenous communities and on all Colombians.

Let us now look at some of the points in the new Constitution which concern us as an indigenous movement.

What importance should be given to constitutional rights?

To begin with, it is a good idea to remember that we, as indigenous people, tied the Constituent Assembly to the 500th anniversary of the invasion of the Americas and a context of crisis for the Colombian State. This crisis was characterized by the illegitimacy of institutions, the discrediting of the political class, the incomplete peace talks, the increase in various forms of violence, the impunity of the authorities, the social tensions provoked by neoliberalism, etc.

The indigenous movement and other groups were criticized for their participation in the Constituent Assembly. Such participation, it was argued, helped to reinforce the State and restore legitimacy to institutions. This point is still being discussed, as is the following question: has the new Constitution really helped to restore legitimacy, overcome violence and achieve the other objectives justifying the convening of the Constituent Assembly?

A fundamental element of ONIC's efforts has been to join its interests with those of other social sectors (other ethnic groups, women, workers, *campesinos*, etc.). Thus, indigenous interventions in the Assembly have not been solely limited to the indigenous question. On the contrary, indigenous people have raised themes such as the forces of public order, the environment, human rights, the state of siege, participation, religion, justice, etc. What has come of this effort to understand other problems and create ties with other social groups?

Indigenous interests were amply covered by the Constituent Assembly. First, the multiethnic and pluricultural character of the Colombian people was recognized. The Constitution also recognizes the rights of indigenous people or communities in the following fields: language and culture; cultural, social and economic integrity; ownership of *resguardos* and communal lands; participation in the harvesting of natural resources; creation of territorial entities enjoying governmental autonomy; sharing of the nation's economic resources; the administration of justice; dual citizenship; special representation in Congress.

The significance of the entrenchment of indigenous rights in the Constitution raised a lot of discussion. However, the following main criticism was made: indigenous participation in this process was equivalent to capitulation. After several centuries of struggle against the State, after preserving their autonomy and character as indigenous societies in South America despite every vicissitude, the

First Nations had surrendered to a State junior to their own. According to this position, it is now meaningless to talk about the problems of acculturation, integration or assimilation into the dominant society since we are already assimilated, thanks to the votes of our own representatives. Some argue that becoming a component of the State through Indigenous Territorial Entities (ETI) is the best evidence that we have been integrated.

Such questions will always exist and are impossible to settle through debate. Nonetheless, it is important to note that there are other possible interpretations of the fact that, for the first time, our rights are entrenched in the Constitution.

This fact implies a great change from previous laws which generally were ignored even by the authorities. These laws were mutually inconsistent and only protected us halfway.

Since they are now enshrined in the Constitution, there is more chance that our rights will be respected. Furthermore, not only our rights are recognized. For the first time on the national level, our full existence is acknowledged, and not as marginal, minority, backward and folkloric societies, as was traditionally the case. It is now recognized that we are distinct peoples, that we are an integral part of the nation, and that our cultures, and especially our attitude concerning nature and preservation of the environment, represent enriching contributions to Colombia.

We believe that this recognition, which is political and not only cultural, is a step forward. From now on, we have the possibility of maintaining our own more autonomous governments within the limits of our territories recognized as ETIs. We should note that ETI autonomy is not absolute, any more than our jurisdictions over justice and education, because we are part of Colombia. It will be necessary to defend autonomy against the practices of the central government if we want to ensure that certain articles of the Constitution do not become straitjackets. This is the case for development plans in the ETI, which must be articulated at the national level. Similarly, customary law must be practised within the framework of Colombian law.

In the past few years, the 82 indigenous peoples of Colombia have been subjected to intense pressure on their territories, resources and cultures, to the extent that the threat of extinction hangs over us. The recognition of our existence and our rights in the Constitution could impede this process. It is easier to dispose of an unknown phenomenon than deal with a question which is now perceived as having national implications.

Let us cite one example which will aid in appreciating the importance of our participation in the Constituent Assembly. The Orinoquia and Amazonia regions, homes to the greatest diversity of indigenous peoples, are coveted by a group of interests which has large-scale plans for development and colonization. To move ahead in this project, they would have to proceed with institutional modernization of these national territories by transforming them into departments. These departments would then be divided into municipalities. If we had not proposed the formula of territorial entities during our participation in the Constituent Assembly, the indigenous peoples of these regions would have been obliged to submit to this "municipalist" scheme.

It is also necessary to specify that the Constitution does not repeal pre-existing laws and decrees which were favourable to our interests. Thus, the main thrust of the legislation affecting indigenous peoples continues to be Law 89 of 1990, which governed the *resguardos*, based on the principle that indigenous peoples were not subject to the Republic's general legislation.

It is also important to note that, at the very time that the new Constitution was promulgated, the Colombian Congress ratified ILO Convention 169. This convention, ratified by Law 21 in 1991, internationally regulates the relations between States and indigenous peoples. This international convention is therefore part of the laws which protect indigenous rights. It would be very useful to communities and regional organization to study Convention 169.

Despite the potential importance of what is written in Law 89, in the Constitution and in Convention 169, our rights have other foundations and we have other recourses not set forth in legislation. This is why we have been able to resist for centuries the efforts deployed to eliminate us physically or culturally. Not only laws count.

As for legal battles, it is not enough to brandish the Constitution in order to win. The laws can remain a dead letter. Government intentions are not the only determining factor. On the contrary, the organization of indigenous peoples and their struggles on the land ensure that the laws are respected.

Legislative power and recognition of indigenous rights

The Congress of the Republic, to which traditional politicians returned after the Constituent Assembly had revoked their mandate, has been quite timid in the recognition of indigenous rights, to the extent that the indigenous Senators even had problems obtaining the right to speak. This situation is reflected in the bills adopted by Congress.

In Law 48 on *conscription*, adopted in 1993, indigenous people were exempted from compulsory military service, but on two conditions: the indigenous person must remain in his territory and abide by the indigenous economic, social and cultural system in its entirety. These conditions mean that indigenous people cannot leave their territories and that the interpretation of these criteria is left to the arbitrary dictates of the military.

In the *Resources and Transfers Law*, indigenous rights have been flouted shamelessly. Indeed, although the Constitution stipulates that municipalities and certain *resguardos* will be entitled to resources from the central government starting in 1994, Congress postponed the effective application date of this right for the *resguardos* until the adoption of a special law.

No mention is made of indigenous territories in the bill on the *National Royalties Fund*, but proposals have been tabled to remedy this omission.

For the *general education* bill, the indigenous Senators had presented proposals developed by ONIC based on the communities' experience. Unfortunately, Congress amended it to such an extent that ethnic education now only exists on paper.

Some proposals were retained from the bill creating the Ministry of the Environment, one of whose reporters was *compañero* Gabriel Muyuy. Two examples were ETI participation in environmental planning and management and indigenous participation in the autonomous regional corporations which will manage the environment.

The laws on *land use planning, dual citizenship* and *police reform* contain provisions on participation by indigenous representatives in certain purely advisory bodies.

The *agrarian reform* bill is becoming a new source of frustration because it does not provide any operational mechanism for significant redistribution of land within the near future, making it a "trickle down" reform. Moreover, this bill replaces State intervention with private initiative. This would make the agrarian reform a lucrative business for landowners. The draft legislation does not provide for administrative expropriation as prescribed in the new Constitution.

It is very important to note that the *Law on the special nature of the San Andrés and Providencia Archipelago* was adopted. Furthermore, the *Law recognizing ownership of land by the Black Communities of the Pacific Basin and other zones of the country* only awaits the President of the Republic's signature. These two laws are a big step forward in the process of constitutional recognition of the rights of indigenous and Black communities.

What about territorial recognition?

The question of territorial recognition is one of those arousing the greatest national interest. It opens the door to a redistribution of power such that the country's political division is no longer based on petty political criteria, as is currently the case, but rather on geographical, ethnic, social, environmental and economic factors. Several groups in Colombia expect a lot from this reorganization. However, the political class has created mechanisms to counteract this reform.

It nonetheless has been observed that grassroots organizations and the *campesinos* have not yet integrated the theme of territorial reorganization into their political analysis. This means that indigenous organizations will have to encourage greater participation by different social forces in a process which concerns them all. It should be noted that, in some cases, even colonists and city dwellers have called for education on these themes.

The reorganization of indigenous territories is making progress, but at a rate that is difficult to assess. While the creation of ETIs has not yet become a subject of national interest in Bogota among decision-makers and the media, this question is fundamentally important in many regions, where it is daily grist for discussion.

In Orinoquia and Amazonia, this theme has aroused great interest, because the population of these regions, a high percentage of which is indigenous, has seen three types of territorial organization imposed in recent years. First came an organization of land ownership which took the area's geography into account when vast *resguar-*

dos, considered to be national territories under trusteeship, were constituted, administered by commissioners and intendants. These great *resguardos* were then transformed into departments. Finally, ETIs are now being created. In addition, there is the question of royalties on the natural resources of these territories, especially petroleum.

The question of territorial reorganization also generated a lot of interest in the Pacific region because of the environmental aspect, the substantial indigenous population and the large number of *resguardos*. Moreover, the region is the target of major resource exploitation projects. Added to this are the procedures already under way to recognize the rights of the region's Black communities to their ancestral territories.

Similarly, on the Atlantic Coast — which the government wants to convert into a single territorial entity — the indigenous territorial reorganization has found its echo in public opinion, resulting in an alliance between the indigenous peoples and the *Costeños*[5] during the Constituent Assembly. People are well aware of the interdepartmental environmental importance of the Sierra Nevada de Santa Marta. The same goes for the geopolitical location and resources of the Wayuu territory in Guajira.

This theme is also on the agenda in the Cauca territory. This is explained both by objective demographic and territorial factors (the largest concentration of indigenous people in the Andean region and a series of resguardos covering a large area) and by the social impact of indigenous struggles and demands. The department's economic development potential is another factor.

As can be seen, the interest in territorial reorganization, born in the regions, is making progress towards the centre of the country.

Territorial reorganization has been a very great priority for ONIC. This is why it has undertaken to speed up its own training programs and to act quickly to fulfil its two contracts to conduct consultations on this question in the communities. The first contract was signed with CORPES in the Orinoquia region and the second with the national government. Other indigenous organizations have subscribed to the latter contract, which has received support from the European Community.

These consultations have produced the following results:

1. An outstanding opportunity for communities to reflect on their present, their future, their resources and their problems;

2. Practice in concerted action within the indigenous movement as a whole;

3. Strengthening of ONIC's local, zone and regional organizations;

4. Strengthening of ONIC's presence in the regions, allowing it to better understand and cope with changes, assume greater responsibilities and thereby acquire better information on the workings of the State, the economy and society;

5. Greater understanding of diversity and intercultural realities;

6. The conviction that this entire approach is only a first step and that ONIC must immediately provide for permanent mechanisms to monitor the entire territorial and regional reorganization;

7. Drafting of a law on the transformation of indigenous territories into territorial entities.

How the government and the Constitutional Court have applied the Constitution to indigenous rights

As we have already mentioned, the advancement of indigenous constitutional rights does not depend solely on legislation, but also on the government and the judiciary.

On the international stage, the government proudly exhibits the Colombian Constitution as a perfect model of recognition of indigenous rights.

At the same time, within the country, INCORA[6] turns a deaf ear to the land claims of our communities; the Ministry of Defence builds military bases on the *resguardos*; the U.S. Air Force sets up radar stations on our land; members of the Police and the Army, suspected of being part of the bands responsible for the Sierra Nevada and Caloto massacres, are exonerated of any blame. Many other examples could be cited. We need only mention the recent violent expulsion of the Chenche Socorro community in the Tolima territory, due to INCORA's decisions. The indigenous movement asked the government to commit itself to the International Year of Indigenous Peoples by proposing a development plan for our communities. But all we obtained was a miserable congratulatory decree.

Since 1991, the movement has asked the government to exempt indigenous organizations from the application of Decree 1407 on legal persons of foundations. Instead of responding favourably, the government issued a new decree establishing a system which made *cabildos*[7] and traditional authorities into forms of associations.

In the Sierra Nevada, the President of the Republic promised that the transfers stipulated by the Constitution would occur on the resguardos. But Congress did not endorse this promise and the right to transfers foundered.

In 1990, the government undertook to compensate the Wayuu community for the harvesting of the Manaure salt marshes by awarding it a 25 percent share of the salt-making company. But in 1993, it displayed Olympian arrogance by cancelling its commitment. The community now would only have the right to charge rent.

Empresa colombiana de Petroleos (ECOPETROL) is carrying out petroleum exploration contracts in indigenous territories without any consideration for the communities or the environment.

The Ministries of Mines, Defence and the Interior have not been able to put a stop to the illegal presence of Colombian and Brazilian miners in the Guainia resguardos. But at the same time the State has helped itself to this department's mineral resources.

Educational and cultural institutions have simply disregarded the constitutional changes. The Ministry of Education has been negligent about resolving the question of contract education.

At ONIC's request, the National Council on Indigenous Policy has been revived. However, our organizations are not represented on this body, which only has parliamentarians as members.

The judiciary and the Constitutional Court have played an important role in the practical interpretation of indigenous rights and the policy changes enshrined in the Constitution.

Thus, thanks to the *acciòn de tutela*, a trusteeship procedure, judges have been able to protect various indigenous communities. Some examples of this are the Embera-Chamis of Cristiania, whose rights have been injured by the construction of a highway on their *resguardo*; the Nukaks whose very lives are threatened by the oil companies' penetration of their Guaviare territory; the Wayuus, who suffer from the pollution produced by coal mines in the Guajira region; the Guananos of Vaupés, who oppose the use of landing strips in their *resguardos* without their communities' authorization; and the Eperara-Siapidaras of Nariño, confronted with INCORA's refusals and delays in their demand for establishment of a *resguardo*.

Constitutional Court judgments are pending in *acciones de tutela* against the destruction of the Bajo Atrato d'Antioquia forest and the installation of U.S. radar stations at Araracuara in the Caqueta region.

The Constitutional Court has declared that the contracts between the government and the Church to provide education in indigenous communities are unconstitutional.

On another front, it should be mentioned that ONIC is campaigning to promote the replacement of "National Language Day," currently celebrated on April 23 of each year, with "a week of all languages spoken in Colombia." Several Departmental Assemblies have recognized indigenous languages as official languages.

Finally, among the consequences of implementing the Constitution, a census of indigenous populations and their housing conditions will be conducted this year for the first time.

Notes

1. The National Organization of Indigenous Peoples of Colombia (ONIC) was created in the early 1970s as an umbrella group of Colombia's regional indigenous federations. During the overhaul of the country's constitution in 1990-1991, it managed to elect a candidate to the Constituent Assembly: Francisco Rojas Birry. This document, written by ONIC, describes the participation of Colombian "ethnic groups" in the National Constituent Assembly, which met in Bogota from February 5 to July 5, 1991. It describes the previous approaches and recalls the constitutional proposals, how they were presented and the peripatetic progress of the Constituent Assembly, in the hope that this assessment may be useful to others.
2. See Appendix V: "Ethnic Groups of Colombia."
3. The *resguardos* are territories reserved for the indigenous peoples. The indigenous peoples have community title to the lands of the *resguardos*. These lands are free of taxes and the people who work them have a full lifetime right of use. There are other reserves in Colombia which belong to the nation.
4. See Appendix VI: "The Rights of Indigenous Peoples and other Ethnic Groups in the New Colombian Constitution."
5. The people of the Coast.
6. INCORA: Colombian Institute for Agrarian Reform.
7. *Cabildos*: popular assembly occasionally convened by the authorities. These assemblies are endowed with decision-making power.

Chapter 4

Kuna Government Autonomy in Panama

by Marie Léger

Most Kunas live on small sand and palm islands in the Caribbean Sea. The forty inhabited islands are part of a reef-protected coral archipelago, located east of the Atlantic entrance to the Panama Canal and extending to the Colombian border. The inhabited islands are densely populated. They generally are near the coast, where the Kunas have their fields, obtain their wood and drinking water and bury their dead. A long strip of land, about 200 kilometres long, bounded on the mainland by a chain of mountains, makes up their territory.

Among the indigenous peoples in Panamanian territory,[1] the Kunas enjoy the greatest political autonomy. Over the years, they have gained recognition for some of their territorial rights and, since 1953, a form of government autonomy. Kuna institutions, including the General Congress, are enshrined in a law which also defines the official borders of their exclusive territory. However, these borders do not encompass all their communities or all of their ancestral territory.

The Kunas' special status has been won through hard struggle, and the protection of their cultural and territorial integrity is a matter of constant concern.

Autonomy Rooted in History

The Kunas have had contact with Europeans for a very long time. The first European visitors to what is now Panama arrived on Columbus' fourth voyage at the beginning of the 16th century. Panama quickly became a strategic transit point for goods heading to and from Spain. From that time on, conflicts between Kunas and Spaniards were incessant. In the 17th century, the Kunas carried their attacks to the gates of Panama City, while the Spaniards undertook various military expeditions into the Darien jungle, where the Amerindians lived. On the spiritual front, Dominican and then Capuchin friars tried to evangelize the natives, but successive revolts put an end to the missions around 1651.

In the late 17th century, the Kunas allied themselves with the buc-caneers who sailed the Caribbean and engaged in trade with them. Together with some Jamaicans, the Kunas also organized an uprising which lasted from 1775 to 1789, during which they attacked the mines of Darien operated by the Spaniards. As certain Kuna accounts reveal,[2] the resistance to the Spanish occupation had its down side: the population was decimated.[3]

At the time of the European arrival, most of the Kunas seem to have inhabited the Colombian jungle, where a few communities still live. After the extermination of the Cueva Indians, they left their original territory and migrated to Darien, only to be pushed further north by the Spanish expeditions and their Embera neighbours. In the mid-19th century, they finally settled on the islands of the San Blas coast, which today is called Kuna Yala.

De facto independence until 1903

In 1821, a new step began when Greater Colombia, of which present-day Panama was a part, gained independence from Spain. The Kunas then attempted to obtain recognition of their sovereignty from the new Republic. In 1871, a decree created an administrative and territorial unit, the *Comarca Tulenega*,[4] with borders that overlap modern Colombia and Panama, governed by a Commissioner General appointed by the executive authority.[5] Although the decree gave the Commissioner the task of protecting the Kunas from external aggression, it clearly fit into the Colombian policy of "civilizing the savages." Nevertheless, this was the first legal recognition of the exist-ence of a Kuna territory.

In fact, until Panama seceded from Colombia in 1903, the Kunas were independent. They escaped virtually any national control and conducted their own foreign trade, mainly with the British.[6] This situa-tion of relative independence would gradually be eroded until the time of the *Revolucion Dule*, as the Kunas themselves call it in Spanish.

The *Revolucion Dule* of 1925

At the beginning of the 20th century, Panama won independence from Greater Colombia with the help of the United States, to support construction of the interoceanic canal. The new State undertook to forge a national identity based on the Castilian language and a Spanish heritage. In the view of successive governments, since the country was ethnically heterogeneous, this difficult task entailed the integration of the indigenous populations.

In 1904, the government began to regulate maritime trade at San Blas and a Jesuit was sent there in 1907 at government expense to begin the work of evangelization. In 1908, the Panamanian government adopted the Indian Civilization Law, the first article of which read as follows: "The purpose will be to reduce the savage tribes which exist in the country to civilized life, by every pacific means," including missions, education, land concessions to non-indigenous colonists, gifts of farm implements, livestock and scholarships.

In 1912, Liberal President Belisario Porras, an anticlerical supported by the popular classes and less pro-American than his Conservative predecessor, cut off government support to the missionaries, but resolutely embarked on a campaign of integration and assimilation.

During his visit to Kuna territory, the Panamanian President was offended that the Kunas considered themselves to be sovereign over their territory:

> Efforts by Cimral Colman [an important Kuna chief] to secure legal title [for his people] for San Blas using funds raised by levying coconut quotas on his villages, which suggested extralegal taxation, offended them even more. Since both sides [Kuna and Panamanian] saw control of the land as essential to their integrity, as a nation or as a people, conflict on this point was inevitable.[7]

Between 1915 and 1925, numerous initiatives reduced the Kunas' leeway. The Panamanian government wanted to recover the unoccupied lands of the San Blas region to its profit. To accomplish this, it created a district destined for colonization. The *Comarca Tulenega* administrative unit, obtained by the Kunas in the time of Greater Colombia, no longer existed. Without consulting the Kunas, the Panamanian government granted concessions to the *Vaccaro Bros* company to operate a manganese mine and to the United Fruit Company for banana plantations. It banned any trade between the Kunas and abroad, even though their economy was based on the trade in coconuts with the Colombians.

A district leader was appointed in San Blas by the executive branch of the Panamanian State. He surrounded himself with policemen to enforce order in the territory. But they also took it upon themselves to arrange the disappearance of anything they considered to be symbols of non-submission to Panamanian sovereignty. They also tried to eliminate everything they considered barbarous, such as nude public bathing, puberty ceremonies for young girls, and the women's clothing and nose rings traditionally worn by Kuna women.

The police also made one Panamanian custom compulsory: Saturday night dances. The physical proximity of the partners in "Western" dances was completely unacceptable to the Kunas. One of the objectives of this imposition seems to have been to encourage marriages between Kunas and Panamanians.

These attacks on the most deep-rooted features of Kuna identity set the match to a powder keg and triggered the *Revolucion Dule*. In February 1925, during the Panamanian carnival, the Kunas revolted, killed twelve policemen of Latin and indigenous origin, six Mestizo children and a few merchants and allies of the police. In all, 27 people were killed.[8] These events lasted a week, at the end of which negotiations with the Panamanian government were held on a ship, the *Cleveland*, in the presence of the U.S. *chargé d'affaires*. A treaty, which some would call a surrender, was then signed, the Treaty of El Parvenir. It must be noted that the Kuna revolutionaries were allied with Richard Marsh, close to the U.S. authorities in Panama, who had made sure of the neutrality of his country of origin. Marsh hoped for the creation of an American protectorate for the Kunas, possibly to facilitate exploitation of natural resources. His hopes would be dashed, but the Kunas would win incipient recognition from the Panamanian State and avoid repression.

The following were the highlights of the treaty which ended the revolt:[9] confirmation of indigenous territorial rights, revocation of concessions, obligation for non-Kunas to obtain the community's consent to spend the night in San Blas, a promise to employ married policemen in the future and to favour access by Kunas to these positions. In exchange, the Kunas recognized Panamanian sovereignty and accepted the introduction of the national education system.

Not all communities signed this treaty, but the effect of its ratification was to end the fighting. Three tendencies then existed among the

Kunas: the first, which favoured some modernism, was made up of three communities most affected by the assimilation measures. Its supporters accepted Panamanian sovereignty and Western culture, called for the abandonment of certain traditions and counted on the protection of the Panamanian State. The second tendency, made up of communities which had remained loyal to Colombia, tried through diplomatic channels to exploit the tensions between Panama and Colombia to obtain an advantage for the Kuna people. The third tendency, initially favourable to the new Republic of Panama, then led the *Revolucion Dule* of 1925.[10]

In 1930, the communities united to send the government a petition in favour of respect for individual rights (particularly the right to vote) and the reserving of all land in the San Blas district for the indigenous people. A few months later, a law was adopted granting reserve status. In 1938, another law created the *Comarca* of San Blas, giving it special administrative status.[11]

In 1945, the first General Congress of the Kuna people met, with the participation of the majority of communities. The General Congress was recognized as the supreme institution of the Kunas and legalized by Law 16 of 1953.

The 1925 revolution has great symbolic importance to the Kunas: it constitutes an essential reference point in the struggle for autonomy and for the preservation of institutions and cultural identity. The protagonists of these events became historical figures who the Kuna people like to evoke as examples of pride and determination.

The *Revolucion Dule* marked a turning point in the relations between the Panamanian State and the Kunas. It confirmed the latter's determination and, to some extent, sealed Panama's acceptance of their special status. The most obvious consequence was the Panamanian State's abandonment of its attempts at rapid assimilation undertaken between 1904 and 1925. A little later, there would be the creation of a reserve and a *Comarca*, officially recognizing some Kuna institutions and legalizing a certain degree of indigenous government autonomy. In exchange, the Kunas henceforth accepted the sovereignty of the Panamanian State over their territory.

The Shape of Autonomy

Even if Panamanian governments have not given up on eventual integration of the indigenous peoples and even if legislation does not yet give them real autonomy, the Kunas nevertheless have acquired leeway that allows them to partially control the development of their territory.

The legislative framework of Kuna autonomy (the 1953 Law) poorly describes its application in daily life. Despite the risks of overlap, the following section first describes the institutions in everyday terms and then presents the legal texts.

Everyday autonomy

Two kinds of institutions govern Kuna life: the traditional institutions created over time by their own design and Panamanian institutions originating from non-Kuna society.

The community is the basis of the Kuna political system. Institutions are primarily village-based. Those which encompass all of the people are made up of representatives of communities rather than of individuals, as in most Western parliaments. To some extent, this is a confederal system, the central institution of which is called the General Congress.

The Panamanian State provides government services in the villages and appoints an intendant to represent the executive authority in the territory.

Kuna local institutions

Discussions and decisions concerning community life take place at the daily sessions of the local Congress, held in the meeting house, the centre of each village's political and spiritual life. Every evening, village leaders gather for ritual chants and to manage the village's daily affairs. The sessions of the local Congress are public and all villagers have the right to speak.

The community's leaders are the *saylas*. There may be two, three or even only one of these. The *saylas* moderate the sessions of the local Congress. Chosen for their great integrity, their sense of the common good and their knowledge of the traditions, the *saylas* generally are of mature age and already have a long track record of learning the rituals and the special ritual language. They have stood out for their ability to serve their community. Most often they are men, but it is said that women have fulfilled this function. They sit in hammocks strung at the centre of the meeting house and on wooden benches set up nearby. The *saylas* are accompanied by *argarganes* who interpret the traditional chants, performed in ritual language, into everyday language for the audience. Assemblies which mainly consist of rituals draw all villagers, but women are often absent from administrative meetings.[12]

In addition to its ritual functions, the local Congress has far-reaching jurisdiction. It organizes economic development and community labour (cleaning the cemetery and the landing strip, building new houses, cultivating collective fields, etc.) and administers justice. Offenders against Kuna rules will be required to perform community labour or pay fines, depending on the gravity of the infraction. In cases of recidivists or very serious offenses, the local Congress may decide to turn the guilty party over to Panamanian justice.

The decisions of the local Congress are made after the villagers have expressed their points of view, the leaders have examined different aspects of the issue debated, heard different opinions and summed up the consensus when it seems to have been reached.

The local Congress sessions are not only ritual or administrative. They also make it possible to prepare for the leaders' activities outside the community, hear their reports or simply listen to stories of people's travels, friends or strangers.

Kuna communities in urban settings

Some members of Kuna communities leave for Colon or Panama City to study or work. When their numbers justify it, some of them open an urban chapter for members of their ethnic group. A courier system makes it possible to send provisions, money or news to Kuna Yala. Under a special tax system, urban residents can pay compensation to their home village if they are absent during community labour. There is also an umbrella group of urban chapters which sends a delegation to the Kuna General Congress.

Health

The Kuna authorities include various specialists in traditional medicine who know medicinal plants and rituals. A significant proportion of the population uses their services.[13]

Traditional education

Traditional education continues to exist in Kuna Yala. It is long, demanding and intimately linked to horticultural activities. But more and more young Kunas study in the Panamanian school system and leave the territory when they want to go beyond secondary education (there are over 400 Kuna university students, most of them boys). In addition, the exodus of part of the work force to urban centres would have the effect of reducing the number of people available for work in the fields and food production. It therefore would become more difficult for the young people who remain in Kuna Yala to free themselves from subsistence activities to devote their time to the study of traditional wisdom.[14]

Kuna "comarcal" institutions

The communities have a lot of contact with each other. Visits are frequent and decisions affecting the whole community are made in common. Two institutions cover all communities: the Cultural General Congress and the Kuna General Congress. They function entirely in the Kuna language.

The Cultural General Congress

The role of the Cultural General Congress is to foster the protection and transmission of the cultural and historical heritage. It brings together members of all communities, particularly their spiritual leaders. A Panamanian sociologist, Raul Leis, has compared it to a Kuna cultural academy.

The Kuna General Congress

The Kuna General Congress is the government of the Kuna people. It is presided over by three *sayladummagan*[15] (the grand *saylas*) from different regions of the territory. The General Congress meets every six months and is made up of delegations of five persons from each community, designated by the local Congresses. Only the principal *sayla* of each community has the right to vote, while the delegates have the right to speak. Nevertheless, most decisions are made by consensus. The General Congress is also attended by delegates of the main Kuna organizations: the Youth Organization, the Canal Workers Association, the Federation of Urban Chapters, certain Kuna non-governmental organizations (research centre, consultants), etc. They have the right to speak but cannot vote. Senior civil servants of the Panamanian government, police representatives and Kuna deputies in the Panamanian Legislative Assembly are also present to answer questions or give information.

Between sessions, the General Congress functions with a permanent Secretariat to which are attached counsellors and five-member volunteer commissions appointed at the meetings: economy, international affairs, projects, education, culture, health and, since 1993, women's issues. Ad hoc committees also may be formed as needed. Thus, in 1993, a committee of three persons from each community was given the responsibility of watching the borders to deal with the problem of the invasion of Kuna territory by colonists. The committee had the mandate to clear the forest along the border, ensure that no colonists settle there and negotiate with people who had already settled there for them to leave.

The General Congress has very broad jurisdiction, ranging from decisions on political orientation to decisions of an administrative, economic or judicial nature. It is difficult to apply the usual branches of government — executive, legislative and judiciary — to the General Congress. This body votes or agrees on resolutions which will have to be applied, whether by a community or by a non-governmental organization.[16] It also occasionally may rule on questions of a judicial nature. To some extent, the permanent Secretariat acts as an executive, in the sense that it ensures follow-up between sessions and prepares themes for discussion at meetings. The voting members of the General Congress are the communities, but the urban social organizations also have a voice. The General Congress brings together all components of Kuna society to decide the questions that affect them, under the direction of the *saylas*. It functions more as a deliberating assembly than as a parliament of the type familiar to Western societies.

Panamanian institutions

Panamanian institutions take several forms: the direct presence of a representative of the executive branch in the territory, the more administrative presence of services offered by government ministries and the deputies elected by the Kunas to the Legislative Assembly in Panama City.

Panamanian institutions in the communities

Government services are present in most villages. These include primary schools, secondary schools in some cases, health centres (three hospitals and sixteen dispensaries or health centres throughout the territory),[17] post offices and, rarely, a police station. They all are accountable to the Ministries concerned in Panama City. The Ministry of Education, for example, controls the budget, plans programs and pays staff. Despite a constitutional provision allowing this, there is no bilingual education for indigenous children. Their curriculum is the same as for the Republic's other schoolchildren and is taught in Spanish. However, since a significant proportion of teachers are of Kuna origin, this allows the *de facto* adaptation of certain courses. In addition, village initiatives to compile traditional oral education for school-age children, funded by international co-operation, are in progress.

The intendant

According to the law, the intendant represents the Panamanian government's executive branch in Kuna territory. He has the power to approve or disapprove the decisions of the General Congress. However, the intendant is chosen by the Panamanian government from a list of three persons elected by the Kuna General Congress, which moderates the power provided by law. The intendant is a Kuna who, to some extent, acts as an intermediary between the Panamanian State apparatus and the traditional structures.

The Kuna representatives in the Legislative Assembly

The Kunas elect three deputies to Panama's Legislative Assembly. In principle, these could constitute Kuna participation in the development of national policies and represent a form of link between the Kuna system and the Panamanian system. However, although they are elected by the Kunas by universal suffrage, the deputies run under the banner of the major national parties. As members of Panamanian parties, the deputies depend on partisan authorities whose positions are developed at the Panamanian national level. Once elected, the deputies find themselves caught between a rock and a hard place, between the decisions of the General Congress to which they are accountable as Kunas and their Panamanian party line, torn between their ethnic allegiance and their partisan affiliation.

In short, the local and General Congresses represent the traditional form of government of the Kuna people. They have authority over a significant part of everyday life. But the Panamanian State offers services which affect everyone's activities. These two types of institutions are sometimes competing and conflictual, sometimes complementary. The real exercise of autonomy depends on the relationship between the two. But the legislative framework is not very precise about each institution's powers.

The legislative framework

The jurisdictional limits of the Kuna and Panamanian institutions present in Kuna territory are laid down in three main legal documents: the Constitution, Law 16 of 1953 and the *Carta Organica*.

The Panamanian Constitution

The articles of the Panamanian Constitution concerning Amerindians were revised in 1972, before the international movements in favour of official recognition of indigenous rights. Only a few articles deal with the First Nations, some to promote the study of their cultures and languages, others to foster participation in national social and political life. Nothing is said about rights or recognition of any special status.

Article 84 of the Constitution indicates that the State will promote programs of bilingual education. This article has never been applied. Only Article 116, the framework for laws on the reserves, defines any real specificity:

> The State shall guarantee the indigenous communities the reserve of necessary lands and the collective ownership of these lands to allow them to achieve economic and social well-being. The law shall regulate the procedures for achieving these objectives, as well as the limits within which private appropriation of land shall be prohibited.

The Constitution thus grants no special recognition to the rights of indigenous people, except for the possibility of a special system of land ownership (Article 116) and a declaration on respect for the ethnic identity of communities (Article 85).

Law 16 organizes the San Blas *Comarca*

Since its adoption in 1953, the Kunas acquired a special status not recognized for the other indigenous peoples of Panama. Indeed, contrary to the Constitution, this law only applies to the Kunas of the San Blas coastal region (Kuna Yala) and not to other peoples or even to the several thousand Kunas living on the mainland outside the limits of San Blas.[18]

The law first establishes the *Comarca* territorial limits, a coastal strip about 200 kilometres long and 15 kilometres wide, plus an archipelago of 300 islands and islets. It then establishes that the higher authority within the territory is held by an intendant, representing the executive branch of the Panamanian government, who is responsible for enforcing the laws, taking care of territorial development, keeping records, etc. (Article 10). It gives the Ministry of Education the responsibility for Education (Article 17) but provides that the indigenous authorities and the intendant will be consulted on the appropriateness of opening new schools.

The core of Bill 16, which sets the limits of the Kunas' leeway, is found in Articles 11, 12, 13 and 21. The authority of the three leaders, the *sayladummagan*, is recognized in the Constitution and the definition of their powers is carried over to the *Carta Organica*. The same goes for the authorities of each community. However, it is specified that the jurisdiction of these authorities must not be incompatible with the Constitution or the laws of the Republic.[19]

The central article of the law, Article 21, "the reserve lands may not be allotted to a person who is not a member of an indigenous community unless it has been specifically approved by two different General Congresses."[20] This article allows the General Congress to approve or disapprove individual or corporate development projects on Kuna Yala territory. In effect, if non-Kuna individuals or companies wish to undertake a resource development project within the borders recognized by law, they must request authorization from the General Congress, which alone has the power to allocate land. Thus, although the Kunas do not legally have ownership of underground resources, they exercise some control over their use.

The *Carta Organica* (the "Fundamental Charter")

This is the third document which completes the Kuna legislative framework. Considered to be the internal constitution, approved by executive decree of the Panamanian government, it clearly defines communal authorities: the local Congresses and the General Congress, the *sayladummagan* and *saylas* of the communities, the *argarganes* and *sualibedis*. It specifies the powers of each and the procedures to be followed in the organization and holding of Congresses.

The General Congress has many powers defined by the existing law: ensuring the well-being and progress of the *Comarca*, preserving its traditions, management of funds, performance of necessary work, etc. The *saylas* are described as the repositories of tradition, the preachers of Kuna religion and doctrine, the leaders and guides of the community. They thus must give preference to general interests over special interests and long-term interests over transient interests. They also must display irreproachable conduct, both public and private.

The *Carta Organica* also stipulates that members of the community must obtain authorization from the authorities to be allocated unoccupied lands. It finally contains a section on the family and tradition.

The *Carta Organica* is important, because it inserts Kuna institutions into the framework of Panamanian legality. In legal terms, to some extent, it provides the regulations for Law 16 of 1953.

In short, the Panamanian Constitution does not recognize the principle of government autonomy, it only includes a few clauses for cultural protection and legalization of collective ownership. Instead, Kuna autonomy is defined by the Panamanian State through legislation. Its most significant elements concern recognition of traditional institutions, even though they have to work under the intendant's authority, and relative control of development through the power of the General Congress to allocate or refuse to allocate land to non-Kunas. This control of the allocation of land is fundamental and no doubt is the most stimulating factor for people thinking about government autonomy.

The Kunas' leeway does not so much depend on the strict interpretation of these legal tools as on the concrete application of certain provisions, the real impact of which is modified. Thus, for example, the commitment of the Panamanian government to choose the intendant from a list submitted by the General Congress represents a change from what is stated in the law.

Two systems, two worlds

For Kunas who live in the communities, autonomy means a number of very specific things: not paying taxes to the Panamanian government, but rather contributing to the collective wealth through community labour, being judged by the traditional authorities and being represented by them to the President of the Republic of Panama, transmitting their property according to tradition, exercising some control over the development of resources, living in Kuna with their compatriots and settling with them their essential problems and the events of daily life.

This autonomy also has limits: attending school in Spanish and learning what Spanish-speaking Panamanians consider it important to know, living with underinvestment in infrastructures and public works and not benefiting from the support of the Panamanian State to market Kuna products.

Autonomy also has social costs: a malnutrition rate twice as high as the national average and an even higher mortality rate.

The margin of autonomy enjoyed by the Kunas has evolved with the relationship between the State and the traditional authorities:

> Every day, conflicts arise between traditional institutions and State structures. The Nation-State, in seeking to divide the *"cacicazgos"* [the traditional territories], has generated antagonisms and constant splits. Even if the Kuna people recognizes the Panamanian State, it aspires to a status of self-determination within Panama. However, in the 1970s and 1980s, incidents and jurisdictional conflicts proliferated between the traditional

authorities and State power and, on many occasions,
the State has ignored the opinions of the Kuna General
Congresses.[21]

Up to now, the Kunas have not obtained self-determination
within the Panamanian State. Moreoever, the State has all the legal
tools to ignore the opinions of the General Congress. Indeed, the law
states that the supreme authority of the *Comarca* is the intendant appointed by Panama. This intendant, designated from a list supplied
by the General Congress, theoretically could play a linking and harmonizing role between government policies and the decisions of the
traditional authorities. However, explicit mechanisms would be
needed to achieve such harmonization.

The other major problem is the absence of financial resources for
the General Congress. The communities collaborate to make it possible to hold Congresses (food, gasoline for boats, lodging, etc.) and
contribute to maintain this institution, but the General Congress does
not benefit from government transfer payments, which limits its
ability to act and obliges it to resort to co-operation projects.

The existing structure therefore poses problems to the extent that
there are two parallel thrusts, that of the Panamanian administration
and that of Kuna tradition. The way in which they clash or comple-
ment each other depends on the people in place and the political
situation.

The strength of the Kunas in their relations with the Panamanian
State also depends on the cohesion they display. If decisions of the
General Congress are not applied by certain communities, if there is
an erosion of traditional structures, then the balance of power is
weakened. If, on the other hand, these communities form a common
front against certain government decisions which go against the will
of the General Congress, it becomes difficult for the State to apply
them.

Some challenges with which the Kunas are confronted certainly
relate to recognition by the State of greater autonomy, but others go
far beyond this. These pertain to the capacity of traditional structures
to meet the requirements of the modern world and to what is being
demanded of minority peoples, in addition to the tensions inherent in
the coexistence of two world-views.

A Proposal for Sovereignty-Association

Unlike many indigenous peoples of the Americas, the Kunas have a territorial base over which they exercise limited autonomy. History has made this territory homogeneous, with no non-indigenous enclaves. Title to this territory is legally recognized, even though the Kunas have to defend it fiercely, and even though its area is insufficient and does not cover all ancestral territory or all Kuna communities. The traditional institutions have not been banned and continue to function to govern many aspects of daily life. The Kunas thus have a base from which they can support an increase in their autonomy and clarify their jurisdictions, to think of their development and their future.

Like many indigenous people of the Americas, however, the Kunas must face very difficult challenges. Forged by a tradition thousands of years old, intimately linked to the tropical forest and horticulture, but under pressure from Panama's Western modernity, this small people is seeking to maintain its identity while it develops, and to change while remaining true to itself. The colonization policies of the Panamanian government are rendering the Kuna territorial base ever more precarious. It is already insufficient to sustain population growth.

The legal framework which currently governs the Kunas was conceived as a concession by the Panamanian Republic, pending their integration into the national whole, and not as recognition of a legitimate right to special status. This poses important problems. The existence of two parallel government structures, the Panamanian State and the General Congress, without any form of co-ordination other than submission to an intendant, has become a straitjacket.

The General Congress therefore decided that it was imperative to change the legal framework, both in terms of the laws defining government autonomy and in terms of constitutional recognition. It began by producing a document that defined the framework for autonomy and submitted it to Panama's Legislative Assembly. The Kunas called this preliminary draft the *Ley fundamental de la Comarca Kuna Yala*, or *Anteproyecto de Ley sobre el régimen especial de la Comarca Kuna Yala*. It would replace both Law 16 of 1953 and the *Carta Organica*.

The content of the proposed basic law

The draft basic law produced by the Kuna General Congress proposes to clarify the power structure within the territory of Kuna Yala.

Increased autonomy

While Law 16 of 1953 entrusted the supreme authority to an intendant appointed by the Panamanian State, Article 4 of the proposed law states that "The communities of the Kuna Yala *Comarca* will be subject to their own authorities which are: a) the Cultural General Congress; b) the Kuna General Congress; c) the *Sayla Dummagan*; d) the Village Congress; e) the *Sayla* ...." Article 9 adds: "The Kuna General Congress is the supreme political and administrative deliberative and decision-making body of the *Comarca*; its adopted positions and resolutions shall be binding on the authorities and villages of the *Comarca*, from the time they are published. Non-compliance with its prescriptions will be subject to sanctions according to the standards established by the statutes of the *Comarca*."

The proposed law also eliminates the obligation for the General Congress to comply with the Constitution and laws of the Republic of Panama, which was contained in Law 16. If these articles were ratified, the subordinate position to Panamanian law would be altered. In legal terms, this would represent a major shift of decision-making power in favour of the General Congress, which would become the government of the *Comarca*.

Better co-ordination

Some of the articles of the proposed law[22] (Articles 14, 38, 39, 42, 43, 53, 57 and 60) provide that the General Congress will ensure the co-ordination of interventions made in its territory. Programs of education, health and economic development would be planned jointly by the General Congress — or committees appointed by it — and the Ministries or agencies of the Panamanian State. Currently conceived in Panama City, these programs henceforth would be developed jointly.

The wording of these articles does not allow precise definition of the fields of each party's jurisdiction, but establishes that services must be planned in a co-ordinated manner that respects the specific character of the Kuna people. The most complete example is that of education (Articles 38 to 44). The proposed law sets the guidelines of an education which will have to be bilingual and contribute to the preservation and development of cultural values and harmonious coexistence with other societies. Within this framework, the authorities of the *Comarca* and the government authorities concerned would jointly plan, organize and carry out educational programs. If the Panamanian Ministry of Education proposed the opening of an educational centre, the General Congress would study the proposal and give its observations. Likewise, educational projects of the *Comarca* would be submitted to the Ministry of Education. The articles dealing with education emphasize the importance of Kuna culture in the curriculum presented by the Ministry of Education. The promotion and implementation of development projects (Article 57), protection of the environment and management of renewable resources (Article 53) would also be handled jointly.

The main government services thus would continue to be welcome, but any project, program or development plan would first be submitted to the General Congress which would be "… empowered to adopt agreements with the national [Panamanian] government" (Article 14). If the proposed law were ratified, the General Congress then would become the co-ordinating centre for all interventions in its territory.

Recognition of a special identity

The proposed law introduces articles to ensure the protection and cultural integrity of the Kunas. In Article 5, the State recognizes and guarantees the existence of the General Congresses. Articles 45 and 46 concern religious practices: "It is recognized that the Ibeorgun religion is the religion of the Kunas and that it will be taught in the schools which operate in the *Comarca*." Article 64 affirms that the State recognizes the ethnic medicine practised in Kuna Yala. Finally, the last article of the proposed law (Article 68) stipulates that weddings celebrated according to Kuna rites will be recognized in the same manner as civil marriages under Panamanian law.

The institution with the most specific responsibility for cultural protection within the territory is the Cultural General Congress. According to the proposed law, it would set the guidelines for scientific activity (Article 48), ensure protection of archaeological sites (Article 47) and authorize Churches wishing to operate in Kuna territory.

Land tenure and natural resources

Articles 49, 50 and 51 are both in continuity with and more precise than the present legislation (Law 16). The lands of the *Comarca* are inalienable and may not be leased. Article 49 adds that they constitute a heritage of the Kuna people and that their acquisition, exploitation or use must be in accordance with customary practices. Moreover, according to Article 51, the proposed law recognizes four types of property: individual, family, group and communal. These properties are acquired by work, inheritance, purchase or compensation. Natural resources, according to Article 52 of the proposed law, would also be part of the heritage of the *Comarca*. They would be protected by the General Congress in co-ordination with the Panamanian authorities concerned (the text says "national") (Article 53). Nevertheless, control over development would be under the exclusive jurisdiction of the General Congress. Article 14 b) specifies "that it will analyze, approve or disapprove and implement the development plans and programs submitted for its consideration."

Justice

The following provisions (Article 66 and 67) concern the administration of justice: "In application of the provisions of the Code of Procedure and the Penal Code, the customary law of the Kuna people and its system of traditional social control shall be taken into account. The *saylas* of the communities may administer justice according to their traditional methods. The persons involved may appeal to a higher authority when they deem it necessary. In case of necessity or when appropriate, the *saylas* may delegate the task to a committee duly approved by the local Congress."

These articles, if ratified, would provide for the existence and application of two judicial systems on Kuna territory. However, the wording is so imprecise that it is impossible to know in which cases the *sayla* would apply customary law and in which cases the Penal Code would apply.

In short, the objective of the draft legislation presented by the Kuna General Congress is to clarify the power structure and ensure an increase in Kuna government autonomy. If it were eventually ratified, the contents of this proposed law would legally guarantee the General Congress a preponderant decision-making role in everything that affects life and development in Kuna Yala. In this sense, it would be possible to speak of sovereignty or, at least, the acquisition of tools to exercise real autonomy. Indeed, according to this proposal, the General Congress would become the place for co-ordination of all interventions in Kuna Yala territory. It would also protect the most important Kuna gain: the ability to exercise some control over development projects affecting their territory. This control would be exercised, in particular, under Article 52, which stipulates that the exploitation and use of resources must respect customary practices, and Article 14, which gives the General Congress decision-making power over plans and programs intended to apply in the territory. It is currently exercised under an article which gives the General Congress the power to allocate or refuse to allocate land to non-Kunas.

The proposed law introduces cultural protection which is currently nonexistent. It thus lays the foundations of harmonization and co-ordination between the Kuna authorities and those of the Panamanian government in the many fields of jurisdiction they share (education, health, protection of the environment, economic development). In fact, for the Kunas, the dream of associated sovereignty takes the form of full and complete recognition of their institutions and their decision-making power in fields which have a direct impact on them. Their affiliation to the Panamanian State is unchallenged. On the contrary, government services are welcome to the extent that they respect Kuna culture. Kuna participation in the development of Panamanian national policies is not contested either.

However, the proposed law is more a definition of a state of mind, a desire for cultural affirmation and collaboration, than a clear distribution of respective jurisdictions. Even though the text implies that there should be a transfer of financial resources from the Panamanian State to Kuna institutions, the way this should be done is never specified.

The main problem posed by this draft legislation is that of its ratification. Indeed, like several other draft bills concerning indigenous communities which had been presented to the Panamanian Legislative Assembly, that of the Kunas has not yet been ratified at the time of writing this text, December 1993. The Kunas allied themselves with the other indigenous peoples of Panama to increase political pressure in favour of their demands.

The Panamanian National Confederation of Indigenous Peoples

The Kuna, Ngöbe-Bugle and Embera-Waunan General Congresses have formed a single co-ordinating body, the Panamanian National Confederation of Indigenous Peoples (CONAPIP). The common objectives concern recognition, protection, consolidation and delimitation of indigenous territories, recognition of government autonomy for peoples who have not yet obtained it (the Ngöbe-Bugles), modernization of the Kuna legislative framework, ratification of ILO Convention 169 and constitutional recognition of Panama's ethnic and cultural diversity.

To speed up the workings of the government apparatus, CONAPIP decided to use pressure tactics. It publicly demanded that the draft legislation be discussed in the Assembly and set a deadline. Once this time limit had expired, it organized two indigenous strike days in May 1993. Kuna Yala was paralyzed, its intendant dismissed and the Pan-American Highway blocked in several places, while simultaneous demonstrations were held in Embera, Kuna and Ngöbe-Bugle. The forces of order reacted with tear gas and arrests. One person died as a result of this police operation.

Heavily covered by the media, these actions, which also received the support of certain bishops, led to the creation of a committee made up of indigenous leaders and government representatives, and then of a Legislative Assembly committee to discuss the proposed legislation. As of December 1993, no conclusions had yet been reached.

By banding together, the indigenous people pose a major problem for the Panamanian government, since some of the draft laws are more difficult to accept than others. The demands of the Ngöbes, more numerous than the Kunas, threaten the power of Panama's big landowners. The Ngöbes live in a territory where considerable financial interests are at stake: large tracts of land are used for livestock, banana plantations, copper mines, hydroelectric dams, etc. The Ngöbes have never obtained the same recognition as the Kunas and their territory is partially occupied by non-indigenous people. The legal boundaries of Ngöbe-Bugle ancestral territories and their legal protection therefore run up against the interests of the big landowners and mining companies.

The Embera-Waunans won the *Comarca* principle for their communities in 1983. Protection of their territories is not complete, however, since several villages remain outside the limits prescribed by law. The Kunas of Madungandi, who live outside of Kuna Yala, see their lands coveted and invaded by colonists. A hydroelectric dam already occupied part of the territory they occupied. They now demand protection of the remaining territory.

The generalized extension of Kuna-style government autonomy to all other indigenous groups is unacceptable to the Panamanian power structure.[23] The government's senior Minister, Mr. Chevalier, declared that the State could not accept additional enclaves on national territory and wished that the indigenous peoples would "incorporate into the development of national life."

CONAPIP also demands constitutional amendments to entrench the existence of Panama's ethnic and cultural diversity. Up to now, as we have seen, the Constitutional articles concerning indigenous peoples are extremely limited. The objective of the First Nations is now to obtain recognition that cultural and ethnic diversity is a fundamental characteristic of the Republic and thereby put an end to explicit attempts at assimilation.

CONAPIP also echoes the demands of the First Nations of Bolivia, Colombia, Ecuador and Chile who have fought for their countries' constitutions to recognize the *multiethnic and pluricultural* character of their States and have abandoned the idea of a homogeneous homeland.

The status of indigenous nations within the Panamanian State is therefore being renegotiated on several levels: protection of territories, laws defining the government autonomy of each people, the Constitution, and the adoption of international standards. The objective of this renegotiation is to recognize and protect the right of these peoples to preserve their identity and develop according to their own character. Autonomy does not mean the shattering of the State to which these peoples are affiliated, but a redefinition.

Conclusion

Because of special geographical and historical factors, the Kunas have obtained an autonomous status which is difficult to apply generally without reconsidering the way the Panamanian State currently functions. This autonomy, however, is a reference point for two main issues: recognition in Panamanian law of the Kunas' own institutions and the possibility they have acquired to exercise control over development projects in their territory.

The reforms they want to apply to the laws defining their autonomy would allow formal recognition of their government, the Kuna General Congress. They undoubtedly would constitute a decisive factor in their ability to meet the imposed challenges of economic and cultural development.

Ratification of such a law would also be an interesting precedent for the continent's other indigenous nations. Recognition of a specifically indigenous system of government and implementation of conditions allowing coexistence with a State in the European tradition would be an inspiration for many.

Personal Account: Because my ancestors were the first to listen to the birds sing[24]

Excerpts from a text by Alban Wagua[25]

"Because I am the owner of this land and my ancestors were the first to listen to the birds sing on this *Abia Yala*,[26] how could a stranger come to steal this land which is our land, tell me where I must live and what borders not to cross? It is I and it is all of us who must say where we intend to live." This is what the Kuna *argar*[27] Olonaidiginia told us at one Kuna Congress.

...

The rulers listen to international financial institutions. Incapable of understanding our awareness of the land, they prefer to degrade it like savages. The rulers of Latin America are illiterate about everything that concerns the roots of this continent; this illiteracy is a sickness. As one Kuna has said: "The presidents hasten to sell off our homeland dirt cheap because they do not know the ancestors and how they obtained this land." No democracy can be built on ignorance so aggressive that it puts its own roots into question. Yet these roots are the alternative solution, not only in legal terms, but in terms of human conviviality.

The government wonders why we need *Comarcas*, why we need the land or reserves, since the Indians are supposed to integrate and the *Comarcas* are only ghettoes of misery? This is as if we asked why the Panamanians need the Canal, since Panamanians are citizens of the world and the Canal benefits the whole world?

Unfortunately, the authorities of our country are a long way from understanding what it means for a people to have a *Comarca*, a territory, a reserve! They speak to us with disturbing spontaneity about integrating the indigenous peoples, but leave us in marginality and poverty because we do not integrate. We would like to answer them from our point of view. In the first place, what type of integration do they mean? Into what system should we integrate as indigenous people? For what purpose? To subject ourselves to the national aims of the dominant class which marginalize the majority of citizens?

And if they speak to us of economic integration, then we, the indigenous peoples of Panama, have more than enough reasons to affirm that the present government, just like its predecessors, has not been concerned in the least about really "integrating" us. It has been content to give us mild sedative, like a form of valium, to put us to sleep. For over 25 years — let the government consult its archives — we, the Kunas, have asked that our coconuts be sold in Panamanian markets. The Kuna region produces about 25 million coconuts per year, but Panama has never bought even one! The Emberas are desperate. They see their plantains rotting because they cannot sell them. They sell them for one balboa a hundred, almost giving them away, while we, the Kunas, are obliged to buy plantains from Colombia at 8 *balboas* a hundred because our lands are not suitable for this cultivation. The Ngöbes produce coffee. With what middlemen are they forced to do business and what support do they receive from the government?

But the government remains deaf: it speaks of integrating the Indians as if this were a matter of bringing black cows into a barn full of brown cows. What it really prefers is that the Kunas continue their "legalized contraband" with Colombia (only Colombian boats buy our coconuts). Thus, we depend on the whims of Colombians who have boats, their economic vicissitudes and clandestine activities. It is small Colombian boats that bring us rice, sugar and coffee. Yet according to Panamanian law, this is contraband. If we were to suffer from collective food poisoning from these products, what law would protect us?

So what type of integration do they want? That the Kunas cease to be Kunas? That the Emberas sell their land and cease to be Emberas? That the Ngöbes cease to demand their own region? That the big landowners, those who pillage the forests, the mining companies who legally steal Ngöbe lands, that all these people dislodge the true owners and force them to beg in the streets of David?

...

Our fathers see Mother Earth as the mother who welcomes, envelopes and humanizes us. The life of our indigenous peoples is reflected in the very strength of the land. The future, the utopia and the life goals of the indigenous peoples are attached to this motherhood of the earth, to the care that they collectively give to it and to the sacred character of Mother Earth. This is why, when the Kunas, the Emberas and the Ngöbes are refused the right to have a *Comarca*, a reserve or a territory, they are not only being refused the source of their food, but the very source of their being, their identity, their history, their religion and their inalienable right to be a people. Mother Earth includes everything that gives men and women their reason to exist and the possibility to be people. She does not only provide them with nourishment.

According to this conception of the indigenous peoples, the perfection of man is only possible thanks to the vitality of Mother Earth, who is also there when the time comes to show us the road the soul must follow after death. This is the source of the filial bond which unites us, as indigenous people, with the land and the forest, and the fraternal bond which ties us to the sons of this Mother, the trees and the animals.

Our fathers cannot level and destroy the forest because the balance maintained with the earth is the only foundation for our balance as people. Nor can indigenous *campesinos* work a *finca* until the soil is exhausted, because the land "needs to rest" so that it can produce other, more abundant fruits later. The forest is our great refrigerator, our hardware store, our market. When we are hungry, we obtain fresh meat; when we need a house, we find the nails and roofs we need; when we fall sick, its roots and leaves care for us. So we must take care of our refrigerator and preserve our pharmacy and our hardware store. Would the White Man like us to take away the refrigerator in which he keeps his family's food? Neither will we allow anyone to steal our refrigerator, our pharmacy or our market.

...

The indigenous peoples' love for the land and their right to possess it — which has given rise to the demands for legal definition of our territories — and the draft legislation adopted by our General Congresses cannot be grasped by the easy path of constitutionality.

The so-called customary standards of the indigenous peoples cannot be understood solely from a legal point of view. The rules by which our peoples live require a comprehensive understanding of the relationship between man and nature, between the possession of matter and the balance of life, between the past experience of the community, projected into the future, and the force of the present, all of this seen through religious structures which give it cohesion. To place these forms of living only in a legal framework is to caricature them. The issue is not one of mawkish sentimentality for Indian peoples but of fair, practical and legal recognition of territories occupied by their real owners and recognition of national structures, the democratic "realization" of States. "The single unified nation, namely the purely geopolitical nation, when absolutely confounded with the State, causes the elimination of diversity. The Indian nation does not only seek the preservation of diversity, but also its reproduction as an essential condition of democratic life."[28]

"We cannot divide the national territory into small pieces," the authorities say in response to demands for indigenous *Comarcas*.

...

Without a legal force that protects our collective land where our cultures can live, the landowners, the big farmers, the colonists, the forest companies and the authorized or clandestine gold prospectors will continue to destroy our forests. So who really is dividing Indian, or so-called national land?

We, the indigenous peoples, cannot and must not allow the few lands that remain to us, after so many exactions and pillagings, to continue to be taken from us. This would not only be the death of our seed, the destruction of our forests and the contamination of our rivers, but something even more serious: our physical and spiritual death as peoples, the death of our religions, our cultures, our fundamental right to be what we want to be on this earth. The relationships that exist between land, religion, identity and history, in the conceptions and practices of our peoples, are so close that the removal of one element means the destruction of the others. This is why our cry is strong, because nobody wants a living death.

All this requires an urgent revision of the constitutions of the Nation-States of *Abia Yala* and must lead to pluriculturalism and multinationality, if we do not wish to continue this history of genocide, "alterocide" and antidemocracy.

Notes

1. See Appendix VII: "The Population of Panama."
2. Mac Chapin (editor), *Pab Igala: Historias de la tradicion Kuna*, Quito, Ed. Abya Yala, 1989.
3. James S. Olson, in *The Indians of Central and South America, an Ethnohistorical Dictionary,* New York, Greenwood Press, 1991, states that there were 700,000 Kunas before the massacres by Pedro Arias de Avila.
4. The text of the law uses the word "Tulenega" but other texts employ "Dulenega." The two spellings come from the same root, "Dule" or "Tule," which designates a Kuna person.
5. Françoise Guionneau-Sinclair, *Legislacion amerindia de Panama*. Centro de Investigaciones Antropologicas de la Universidad de Panama, Facultad de Humanidades, Universidad de Panama, 1991, p. 12.
6. James Howe, "An Ideological Triangle: The Struggle over San Blas Kuna Culture, 1915-1925," pp. 19-52, in *Nation-States and Indians in Latin America*, edited by Greg Urban and Joel Sherzer, Austin University Press, 1991, p. 20.
7. James Howe, op. cit., p. 30.
8. Ricardo Falla, *Historia Kuna, Historia Rebelde, la articulacion del Archipiélago a la nacion panamena*, Ed. de Capacitacion social, Panama, Serie el Indio Panameno, p. 63.
9. The reference to the text of this Treaty is found in an article by Alexander Moore. However, another author, Ricardo Falla, mentions that the instigators of the *Revolucion* were absent from the signing ceremony and that companies which had obtained concessions prior to 1925 did not withdraw from the territory.
10. Guionneau-Sinclair, op. cit., p. 13.
11. The "reserve" in Panama refers to a type of land ownership (collective and inalienable). The *Comarca* is a reserve in terms of land ownership but has a special administrative system. Under the 1938 law, an intendant was appointed by the executive branch of the Panamanian State. In 1953, the administrative provisions of the *Comarca* were amended to recognize some indigenous institutions.
12. Joel Sherzer, *Formas del Habla Kuna. Una perspectiva etnografica*. Quito, Ed. Abya Yala, Collection "500 anos," 1992. In May 1993, in the community of Carti Suitupo, women were specially convened in the morning to inform them of the indigenous demonstrations which would take place throughout the country. The leaders hoped to have the entire community participate in the movement.
13. *Colon y Kuna Yala, desafio para la iglesia y el gobierno*, Diocesis misionera de Colon, Instituto de Estudios Nacionales, Universidad de Panama, 1992, 318 pp.

14. Mac Chapin, "Losing the Way of the Great Father," *New Scientist*, August 10, 1991, pp. 40-44.

15. *"Sahila Tummat"* or *"Sayladummad"* (*"sayladummagan"* in plural) is written to designate the Kuna leaders. This text adopts the spelling used by the internal bylaws of the 1993 General Kuna Congress.

16. For example, the General Congress mandated a Kuna non-governmental organization to attempt to obtain a patent for *molas*, the embroidery made by Kuna women according to the reversed appliqué technique. The objective is to protect one of their main sources of income against companies which copy Kuna art for mass production intended for foreign markets, particularly Asia.

17. Diocesis misionera de Colon, op. cit.

18. A Kuna territory known as Madungandi exists on the mainland beyond the San Blas cordillera. It is not included within the legal limits of the Kuna *Comarca* and does not enjoy the same protections, rendering it more vulnerable to the incursions of colonists and development projects.

19. The text reads as follows: *"El Estado reconoce la existencia y jurisdiccion en los asuntos concernientes a infracciones legales, exceptuando la referente a la aplicación de la leyes penales, del Congreso General Kuna, de los Congresos de pueblos y tribus, con arreglo a su tradición y de la Carta Organica del regimen Comunal Indígena de San Blas. Dicha Carta tendrá fuerza de ley una vez que la apruebe el Organo Ejecutivo, luego de establecer que no pugna con la Constitución y las leyes de la República."* ("The State recognizes the existence and jurisdiction of the Kuna General Congress for matters which concern offences against the laws — except for the application of penal laws — of the village and tribal Congresses according to their tradition and the *Carta Organica* of the indigenous communal system of San Blas. This charter will have force of law as soon as it is approved by the executive branch, after establishing that it is not contrary to the Constitution or the laws of the Republic.")

20. *"No se adjudicarán tierras ubicadas dentro de las reservas indígenas a ninguna persona que no forma parte de la comunidad salvo que sean aprobadas por solicitudes de adjudicación por dos Congresos diferentes."*

21. Diocesis misionera de Colón, op. cit., p. 21.

22. See Appendix VIII, "Powers of the Kuna General Congress according to the proposed basic law of the Kuna Yala Comarca."

23. *La Prensa*, May 19, 1993.

24. This text is a translation of excerpts from a book by Aiban Wagua entitled: *Para qué Comarcas para los Indios si ellos no trabajan?*, Ed. CONAPIP, 1993.

25. The author is a writer and poet. A priest with a degree from the Salesian University of Rome, he is a member of the International Commission of the Kuna General Congress.

26. Amerindian word meaning America.

27. The *argar* is the interpreter of the ritual language used by Kuna leaders. He explains in everyday language the meaning of the ritual language used by the *sayla* in his speeches.

28. F. Mires, "Nacion e Indianidad: les movimientos sociales indígenas y la cuestión nacional en America Latina," ALAI, August 1992, Separata: IV.

Chapter 5

The Indians of Brazil: A Fragile Constitutional Recognition

Brazil adopted a new constitution in 1988. After a series of pressures, the part concerning "Indians"[1] allowed recognition of some of the rights of the First Nations. However, these constitutional gains are fragile and threatened by those who covet indigenous territories. The political crisis triggered by the fall of President Collor de Mello did not impede a fierce congressional struggle to modify the legislation concerning Indians. The essay by Beatriz Perrone-Moisés presents the context and the new 1988 Constitution, while Paulo Machado Guimaraes focuses on the debates around the legislation on Amerindian peoples.

The 1988 Constitutional Battle

by Beatriz Perrone-Moisés[2]

In 1987, representatives of several of Brazil's Indian nations gathered in front of the National Congress in Brasilia, during the debate on the draft chapter of the Constitution entitled *On Indians*. They thus brought visibility to their recent presence on the national political scene.

The Indians demonstrated on several occasions during the deliberations of the Constituent Assembly. Their participation in the constitutional debate marked a turning point in the historical relationship between the State and the indigenous peoples of Brazil. In fact, they had begun to organize barely fifteen years earlier to fight for their rights, with the support of supportive associations in civil society, the Catholic Church (through the Missionary Indigenist Council, CIMI) and anthropologists.

There are currently some 250,000 Indians in Brazil, members of 200 different ethnic groups and speaking almost as many languages or dialects. They are divided into two main groups (Gê and Tupi), twelve families (Carib, Arawak, Pano, Tukano, Katukina, Puinave, Yanomami, Mura, Txapucura, Takana, Nambikwara and Guaykuru) and thirty languages or language families with very little geographical distribution. These groups, generally small in number, are scattered throughout Brazilian territory (8,511,965 square kilometres), with relative concentration in Amazonia, particularly in the border regions.[3]

These survivors of a population of several million, who lived in the region when the first Portuguese colonists arrived in the 16th century, now exist in a great diversity of situations. Some have been in contact with Whites for centuries; others, whose existence was unknown until a few years ago, are still isolated.[4]

Dispersed among 150 million Brazilians, the Indians are very few in number. Yet in absolute terms, the Indian population has grown in recent years. This demographic growth has lent strength to the movement revising the fatalistic ideology which had marked the Indian question until very recently.

Before this reappearance of Brazilian Indians during the Constituent Assembly in 1987, history books considered them to be doomed. Woeful anthropologists focused their research on the theme of acculturation and cultural change. Because of their physical and cultural fragility, it was assumed, the Indian peoples could not cope with a State which had never recognized their right to be different and which wanted to remake them into non-Indians.

In the 1970s, the ideology of assimilation was strengthened by the major development projects conceived by the military governments: opening of highways, hydroelectric dams, projects to colonize and exploit natural resources in Amazonia. The impact of these projects on the Indians was catastrophic. The Indians' demographic importance and the size of the territory they occupied diminished rapidly as the megaprojects reached the last isolated people in the country. A systematic invasion of Indian lands began. Within a few years, epidemics ravaged entire populations. Those whom the official ideology considered as obstacles to progress, enclaves of primitivism impeding the country's modernization, were caught up under the march of progress.[5]

Since the process of demographic, territorial and cultural reduction was already four centuries old, it was believed that the Indians were on the road to extinction. Their descendants would end up being assimilated by the mass of the population, thus achieving the objective, not of the laws, but of the policy toward indigenous populations in force since the colonial period. In 1987, many

Brazilians were surprised to discover them so alive and active. Despite everything, the Indians had survived.

Peoples afflicted with relative incapacity

In 1987, at the time of the Constituent Assembly, the provisions concerning the Indians of Brazil were scattered through the 1969 Constitution, the Civil Code, Law 6001, known as the Indian Status Act (1973), many ordinary laws adopted by Congress, executive decrees and international agreements signed by Brazil. Until the 19th century, the Indian question, to all intents and purposes, was a question of manpower. It then became a question of territories: those which could be put to use, and especially those with extremely rich underground mineral deposits.

In these laws, the Indians were likened to minors and the mentally handicapped. Under what was termed their "relative incapacity," Indians were under the trusteeship of the State, exercised through the National Indian Foundation, FUNAI. Created in 1967, this agency was responsible for protecting the Indians and their lands, and for promoting their integration into national society. Once integrated, that is, considered as capable of establishing political and economic relations with non-Indians in an autonomous manner without a trustee's intervention, the individuals or communities could be emancipated. As full citizens, they would risk losing their territorial rights, according to one possible but erroneous interpretation of the laws, which would link the land to their civil status of relative incapacity.

The Indian Status Act presented a typology which classified Indians as "isolated," "in the process of integration" or "integrated." Thanks to this dubious interpretation of the laws, many big landowners tried to legitimize their occupation of Indian territories by alleging that the former owners were no longer "real" Indians and thus no longer had any right to these territories. On many occasions, the State itself undertook to restrict the definition of Indian status.

In 1980, the State proposed criteria to determine who was and who was not an Indian in Brazil. This attempt, frustrated by the major protests it aroused, had the multiple aim of suppressing territorial rights, exempting the State from its duties as guardian and silencing certain representatives of Indian movements who had become annoying.[6]

Since territorial rights were linked to relative incapacity, individuals and communities never asked to be emancipated. But governments made several attempts from the 1970s to decree emancipation of individuals or communities without their knowledge, under variable and dubious criteria of "Indianhood."

Until 1988, Brazilian law, therefore, postulated the integration of indigenous people into national society as the central objective of indigenist policy. In the 1934, 1946 and 1967 Constitutions, the indigenous people were called *silvicolas* (forest dwellers) and the State was responsible for "incorporating them into the national community." Article 1 of the Indian Status Act stipulated that: "This law settles the legal status of Indians or *silvicolas* and Indian communities, having the objective of preserving their culture and integrating them in a progressive and harmonious manner into the national community."

The integration to which the laws made reference could be seen as a sign of articulation in a multiethnic society in which these communities and their members could take part, without having to deny their cultural differences or lose their own rights. However, when the term "integration" was interpreted by the big economic and military interests, it translated in practice into assimilation or annihilation of cultural differences and, in the final analysis, sought to make the subjects of territorial rights disappear.[7]

Indian lands, the central problem, were defined by the 1969 Constitution as those occupied by Indians (Article 4). Article 198 recognized their *right to the exclusive use of the natural wealth* found in their territories. Article 17 of the Indian Status Act considered Indian lands, according to the Constitution, to be those "occupied or inhabited by *silvicolas*," while Article 23 specified that "effective occupation of the land he holds according to tribal customs and traditions and where he lives or engages in an activity which is indispensable to his subsistence or economically useful shall be considered as the possession of the Indian or *silvicola*."

This definition of rights to the soil already posed problems, for example, when territories indispensable for hunting and gathering were difficult to occupy effectively or permanently. The question of rights to the sub-surface was even more complicated. The sub-surface of the Indian territories, particularly in Amazonia, is very rich in ore. Its exploitation by non-Indians is one of the greatest problems,[8] not only in legislative terms, but especially in terms of the policy applied by governments in recent years.

The Constituent Assembly

The Union of Indian Nations (UNI) was created in the early 1980s to organize Indian resistance throughout Brazil. In 1987, many other regional and local organizations joined it. Organized for the first time and benefiting from the support of lawyers, anthropologists, members of Congress, the Church and NGOs, the Indians could make their voices heard.

During the deliberations of the Constituent Assembly and under UNI's co-ordination, a popular front was organized around five key issues:

1. Recognition of the territorial rights of Indians as the first inhabitants of Brazil;

2. Demarcation and guaranteeing of Indian lands;

3. The exclusive right of Indian peoples to benefit from use of the natural wealth of the soil and sub-surface of their territories;

4. The transfer, under dignified and fair conditions, of poor workers found in Indian territory;

5. Recognition and respect for the social and cultural organizations of the Indian peoples and their own future projects, and full guarantees of citizenship.

The mobilization of civil society in favour of the rights of indigenous peoples very soon aroused a strong reaction. In 1987, a campaign in the conservative press denounced the alleged conspiracy against national sovereignty by the big mining multinationals, CIMI and all the defenders of the Indian cause. The accusation was so serious that a congressional commission of inquiry was established to clarify the question. Even though the commission concluded that the allegedly incriminating documents were false, this story affected the Constituent Assembly's work, causing it to backtrack on certain points of the initial text, especially those that concerned mining rights on Indian lands.[9]

The strong mobilization by the Indian peoples, particularly the Kayapos and the indigenist associations, made it possible to recover some of the gains of the initial document, but the compromise they had to make remained, as Carneiro da Cunha expressed it, as scars in the final version. All things considered, the 1988 Constitution nonetheless represents remarkable progress towards recognition of the rights of indigenous peoples in Brazil.

The 1988 Constitution

In the 1988 Constitution, the rights of the Indian peoples are covered in different chapters: in Chapter VIII of the section on social order, entitled *On Indians,* and in an article of the Transitional Constitutional Provisions.[10]

Compared to previous laws, this document gives much more importance to the definition of the rights of Indian peoples, which are discussed exhaustively.

The rights of indigenous peoples to their lands are declared to be "original" or inherent rights and thus recognized as predating their acknowledgment by the Brazilian State. Indian lands, only lately defined as lands permanently occupied by them, are now defined in broader terms which take into account the culturally different ways of occupying a territory (Article 231). Previously, the decision to grant permits to exploit water and mineral resources on Indian land was reserved for the executive branch; henceforth, it exclusively belongs to Congress (Article 49). It is also Congress which decides on displacement of indigenous groups (Article 231.5). Transitional constitutional provisions (Article 67) set a five-year deadline after the Constitution's proclamation on October 5, 1988 to mark the boundaries of all Indian lands.

The Constitution makes no reference to State trusteeship. Only the Indian Status Act mentions it. However, since 1991, work has proceeded on drafting a replacement for this law which is more suited to the new Constitution. In fact, Indian resistance prevented the Constitution from mentioning the government agency (FUNAI) in charge of the Indian question. Instead, the Constitution makes the Federal Union the direct spokesman of the indigenous peoples in their relations with national society. In addition, the jurisdiction of legislative and judicial authorities over Indian rights is expanded considerably in the new text.

For the first time, the Constitution recognizes the capacity of Indians, their communities or their organizations to appear in court on their own behalf (Article 232). This is a step beyond trusteeship. The Public Ministry henceforth is responsible for defending the rights of Indian peoples (Articles 129 and 232). This change is fundamentally important, because the Public Ministry is independent of the government in power, meaning that trials relating to Indian rights will be protected from the pressure of special political interests. These are two extremely important gains for the Indians' struggle.

The practice of assimilation, authorized by the interpretation of the term "integration" in previous laws, is finally discarded by the 1988 Constitution. On the contrary, this establishes the protection of manifestations of indigenous culture (Article 215) and recognizes "the social organization, customs, languages, beliefs and traditions" of the Indians (Article 231). They are also guaranteed primary education in their mother tongue and in Portuguese (Article 210). What the Constitution ultimately establishes is the right to be different.

Implementation of the new Constitution

However, the positive provisions of the 1988 Constitution regarding indigenous rights have faced a whole series of obstacles since its proclamation.

The Constitution refers the application of certain articles to complementary future laws. The absence of such laws has allowed the executive branch to resist application of the constitutional provisions on many occasions. In 1990, for example, it even proposed the emancipation of all Indians, the division of trusteeship into two parts, one civil and the other public, and the subjection of the demarcation of Indian lands to various considerations of a non-legal nature. These proposals were clearly unconstitutional.

While trusteeship has vanished from the text of the Constitution and is absent from the drafts of the new Statute of Indigenous Societies, the indigenist policy has maintained its assimilationist spirit. In Amazonia, the interference of the Advisory Secretariat of National Defence, the advisory body directly attached to the President of the Republic and made up of military officers — continues to be powerful.

"Faced with the rise of the democratic movement of the 1980s, the military are seeking to perpetuate their trusteeship over Amazonian development in order to guarantee the opening of the last Indian lands in the region to private interests who hope to exploit their natural resources, through a *fait accompli* which defies the new constitutional authority."[11] National sovereignty, so often invoked against the demarcation of Indian territories in border regions, has resurfaced in the efforts currently deployed to nullify the decree defining Yanomami territory.

Yet in 1989, this same territory had been dismembered into 19 isolated tracts of Indian land, split up by "a national park and national forests" subject to eventual economic exploitation. The act of demarcation of this territory, decreed in 1992 on the eve of the United Nations Conference on the Environment and Development, held in Rio de Janeiro, was considered as a primarily political gesture.

In 1987, Indian territories only represented 8 percent of the country's usable land. Despite this reduced percentage, the accusation has always been made, and echoed in public opinion, that the demarcation was excessive for so few people. On many occasions, during the demarcation process in Amazonia, the media presented comparative calculations, concluding that a territory as large as a European country was being proposed for a population smaller than that of a Sao Paulo neighbourhood. The vast Indian territories of the Rio Negro region (Western Amazonia), located in border regions, are likely to be dismembered into micro-reserves, just like those of the Yanomamis.

The deadline for the demarcation of Indian lands had been set for October 5, 1993. It was not respected.[12]

There were four demarcation steps defined by Presidential Decree no 22 of February 22, 1991:

1. Determination of the limits proposed by a working group, with the agreement of the Indian community concerned;
2. Physical delimitation of the boundaries approved by the Minister of Justice at the end of the previous step;
3. Homologation of the demarcation by presidential decree;
4. Regularization in the official register.

In June 1993, Indian lands in Brazil had the following legal status, according to CEDI:

Status	Quantity	Percentage
Undetermined	106	20.4
Determined	61	11.7
Delimited	101	19.5
Homologated	164	31.6
Regularized	87	16.8
Total	**519**	**100.0**

However, there is a risk that the rights of Indians to their territories will not be respected, even in the case of homologated lands. The rich sub-surface of these territories is defined by Article 176 of the Constitution as "property distinct from the soil." The State therefore reserves the right to exploit them through concessions which it will grant solely to Brazilians or Brazilian enterprises. The sub-surface therefore continues to be the object of pressure from economic groups. Requests for mining concessions in Indian territory are currently paralyzed, due to a lack of applicable regulations.

The sanitation assistance provided by FUNAI (not mentioned in the Constitution, it must be remembered) has never been effective, especially in regions where the massive presence of non-Indians, because of gold prospecting or government megaprojects, has caused major epidemics. Also, FUNAI's powers over health and education have been transferred to the Ministries of Health and Education. These services have not yet been reorganized adequately.

The dangers of constitutional revision

The rights of Indian populations, as guaranteed by the 1988 Constitution, currently run the risk of being limited or even abrogated. The text provided for the possibility of constitutional revision after 5 years, namely as of October 5, 1993. The Constitution may be discussed, not by a Constituent Assembly, but by the Legislative Assembly and the Senate which can introduce amendments. Jurists do not agree on the legal possibility of revision of the entire text of the Constitution. However, it is quite possible that articles concerning the rights of indigenous peoples will be reviewed in any case.

There certainly will be rediscussion of the exploitation of mines and other natural wealth (wood, water resources, etc.). The role of the Public Ministry in the defence of Indian rights, the importance of which has been manifested in the past five years, may also be subject to revision.

This revision, marked by economic and political interests and carried out by a Legislative Assembly, the majority of whose members come from States in Amazonia, where the anti-Indian lobbies are very powerful, will surely not favour Indians. The continuous absence of any definition of a new Indian status may also favour the legal limitation of the rights guaranteed by the Constitution.

To deal with this revision, it will be necessary for Indian organizations, now close to a hundred of them, to unite around a common program. Indians and all those struggling in alliance with them must form a common front to shift public opinion towards guarantees for established rights. The struggle of Indians in Brazil is a recent one that is far from over.

The Stakes of Indian Legislation

by Paulo Machado Guimaraes[13]

Fragile constitutional gains

The provisions concerning Indians in the new Brazilian federal Constitution came out of one of the most hard-fought confrontations between the political groups of the Constituent Assembly. Subjected to unprecedented and salutary pressure from the indigenous nations, these groups established relations between the State and these nations on the basis of completely positive parameters. Let us recall a few of these:

a) The elimination of the perspective of integration of Indians into "national society," present in Brazilian legislation since the beginning of the century, is very important. Thanks to this change, the State and all citizens henceforth must respect and protect the Indians' ethnic and cultural universe.

b) Constitutional recognition of the social organization, customs, languages, beliefs, traditions and ancestral rights of Indians in the territories they traditionally occupy serves as a constitutional beacon of a truly democratic State in which the various ethnic groups are not forced to integrate into the dominant ethnic and cultural reality. Based on the elements recognized in the statement of principles (*caput*) of Article 231 of the Constitution, it may be considered that the constituting authority has implicitly admitted the existence of several nations within the Brazilian State, which means, among other things, that Indians are granted autonomy over their territories.

c) The reduced importance of the central authority as the State's main representative on indigenous questions is another significant aspect of the new Constitution. Since its proclamation, the legislative authority and the federal Public Ministry have acquired an important role in the relationship between the State and the indigenous peoples.

d) The exploitation of water resources and their energy potential, prospecting and exploitation of mineral wealth in Indian territory, like the provisional displacement of indigenous groups in case of a plague or epidemic which endangers the population or in the interest of national sovereignty, now requires the approval of the National Congress.

e) It is also important to point out that only the federal legislative authority may impose restrictions on the rights of Indians over their territories, which undoubtedly will allow for a greater debate on these questions, contrary to the previous practice. Not only did the former constitutional text limit the rights of Indians, but it reserved all decisions which directly or indirectly affected them to the executive branch.

f) The federal Public Ministry assumes the role of "judicially defending the rights and interests of the Indian peoples."

However, despite these institutional gains, the public administration has been most reticent to bring its conduct into line with the new legal principles. It continues to act in complete disregard of the Indians, as if their wishes had no legal significance. At the same time, it continues to decree regulations or adhere to standards which no longer correspond to the new constitutional order.

This resistance exists because the political groups which rule the country now oppose the application of the Constitution. They banded together during the Constituent Assembly to propose the worst text in Brazil's legislative history concerning Indians. Having been isolated politically, this reactionary movement is now trying by force to impose concepts harmful to the Indian peoples and diametrically opposed to the orientation of the new Constitution.

Political context of legislative changes concerning Indians

Like his predecessor, President Collor de Mello, at the start of his term, had not established any policy concerning Indians. Later, Decree 99.405 of July 19, 1990 created an Interministerial Working Group (GTI) with a mandate to prepare measures intended to make the federal government more efficient in preserving and defending the rights and interests of Indian peoples.

The GTI only began its work two months later and completed it in November 1990. It put forward several proposals on the role of the State in the protection of Indian peoples and on the agrarian question, the environment, subsistence, education and health.

Because it did not reflect the thinking of the Brazilian pro-Indian NGO community and represented a serious risk to the integrity of the rights and interests of Indians, the *Açao para ã cidadania* group, a collection of progressive elected representatives and organizations, held a seminar on Indian rights, with the support of the federal Public Ministry, during which participants expressed their disagreement with the GTI's conclusions.

The government was criticized for inefficiency in physical delimitation of Indian territories, especially those traditionally occupied by the Yanomamis. Eight and a half months later, it declared that it could not act until Decree 94,945/87, which established the administrative procedure for demarcation of these territories, was adapted to the country's new administrative reality, since the agencies foreseen for its implementation had been eliminated.

Probably motivated by the loss of political support due to his inaction, Collor de Mello mandated another committee to draft a new administrative procedure within 30 days for physical delimitation of Indian territories (Decree 99,971 of January 3, 1991).

When this deadline expired, five new decrees were promulgated, indicating mitigated acceptance of some of the proposals in the final GTI report. They concerned:

- procedural standards for physical delimitation of Indian territories;
- parameters for medical assistance to Indian peoples;
- actions to protect the environment in Indian territory;
- programs and projects to ensure the economic autonomy of the Indian peoples;
- Indian education.

These April 1991 decrees (22 to 26) entrusted the Ministry of Justice, the National Health Foundation, the Secretariat for the Environment (SEMAM), the Brazilian Institute for the Environment (IBAMA), the Federal Agricultural Research Agency (EMBRAPA) and the Minis-

try of Education and Culture (MEC) with the respective responsibilities for physical delimitation of Indian territories, medical assistance, environmental protection, Indian economic autonomy and
Indian education.

However, these measures were in violation of paragraph XI of Article 48 of the federal Constitution, which established the jurisdiction
of the national Congress over "the powers of ministries and agencies
of the Public Administration," and thus were unconstitutional. In addition to this important problem, these same decrees created an administrative impasse which is still unresolved.

Indeed, by assigning these responsibilities to the above-men-
tioned agencies, the President of the Republic simply took them away
from the jurisdiction of FUNAI (the Brazilian Department of Indian
Affairs currently under the responsibility of the Ministry of Justice),
only leaving it the task of determining the territories traditionally occupied by the Indians, policing these territories and co-operating
with the agencies which had received these new powers. Moreover,
no body was created to co-ordinate the various agencies likely to
operate on the same indigenous reserve, which could hamper the ef-
ficiency of their actions. Since the agencies which had received the
new responsibilities did not have financial resources, let alone
capable personnel — except for the National Health Foundation and
SEMAM, which have intervened in a number of cases, including the
Yanomamis, the Tikunas and the Kaiowas-Guaranis — work with the
Amerindians came to a halt.

At the same time, Decree no 27 gave the same committee "the
power to propose revision of the Indian Status Act and its applicable
regulations, given the provisions of the 1988 Constitution."

In May 1991, this Committee concluded its work. Its proposed
legislation was made public the following June 12. The bill was strongly criticized by the Indians and by the NGOs working with them.

For the first time in Brazil's history, dozens of Indian leaders,
meeting in Brasilia, discussed and formulated their observations on
the rules which should guide relations between the Indian peoples
and the State. On June 20, 1991, they transmitted their criticisms and
suggestions to the national Congress and the federal government.

Since the few efforts devoted to physical delimitation of indigenous territories undermined the government's credibility, the
President of FUNAI was relieved of his duties by the Minister of Justice. This was announced to the public on June 21, 1991, at an

audience granted to a delegation of indigenous leaders who had participated in the Brasilia meeting.

The day before the bill was tabled in Congress, the *Nucleo de Direitos Indígenas* (NDI[14]) presented another bill, called the Indian Societies Law, through their congressional allies.

Before the Congress adjourned, its President, Congressman Ibsen Pinheiro, instituted a special committee to evaluate the new bills. Made up of elected representatives opposed to recognition of the rights of Indian peoples, it elected the representative from the State of Roraima, Teresa Jucá (wife of the former president of FUNAI, Romero Jucá Filho) to report its decisions.

The year 1991 ended in a climate of great tension because of the decision by the President of the Republic to order the physical delimitation of the territory traditionally occupied by the Yanomami people. The government had already met in October to resolve this question and Collor de Mello, giving in to pressure from the military ministers, had decided to redefine the limits of Yanomami territory. Less than a month later, faced with international reaction and fearing pressure from environmental, Indian and pro-Indian movements, he backtracked and ordered the boundaries to be set, going against the military forces and the conservative sections of the national Congress. Collor de Mello feared that these movements would push the governments of their respective countries not to participate in the United Nations Conference on the Environment and Development, scheduled for June 1992 in Rio de Janeiro.

Because of the congressional reactions against the Indians, some progressive political and congressional forces began to act cautiously and reconsidered the extension of Yanomami territory and its location on Brazil's border with Venezuela, as the military already had done. These progressive and popular groups considered that Collor de Mello's attitude represented the victory of international economic interests and imperialist forces who coveted the riches of the Amazon region.

Thus, on the question of Indian rights, the military, the conservatives and the progressive groups, motivated by distinct reasons, used the same argument to achieve different objectives.

The military, allied with right-wing forces in the States of Roraima and Amazonia, made every effort to prevent the physical delimitation of Indian territories considered to be too big or located near national borders. The elected representatives from the State of

Roraima even proposed the creation of a congressional committee funded by the military ministries to investigate the activities of gold prospectors, the existence of clandestine trails and the activities of religious missions in the Amazon region, because they suspected that these groups wanted Amazonia "internationalized."

Anti-Indian forces continue to be structured and active

Early in 1992, the federal government had not yet followed up on the project for defining the indigenous territories. The previous year's decision to define Yanomami territory had triggered very negative reactions from voters in certain districts. Several elected representatives, including those from the States of Roraima and Amazonia, had announced that they would take the necessary measures to block approval of the funds intended for defining these boundaries and the removal of invaders, especially in the Yanomami region.

In addition to this initiative, Congressman Jair Bolsonaro of the Rio de Janeiro Christian Democratic Party presented a bill in March 1992 which revoked Ministerial Decree no 580/91 of the Minister of Justice. This decree defined the limits of the territory traditionally occupied by the Yanomamis. This initiative was part of the pressure tactics launched by the military, both in the reserve and in active service, allied with right-wing political forces.

In May 1992, despite Article 49-V of the Constitution, the National Defence Committee studied and approved Jair Bolsonaro's bill, thus supporting the Congressman reporting on this matter, Abelardo Lupian, who recommended its adoption.

In June 1992, the National Defence Committee organized a seminar on "the army and national defence." The political and strategic analysis of the military proved to have many points in common with that of the Left with respect to imperialist interests on part of Brazil's territory.

The United Nations Conference on the Environment and Development (ECO-92 or the Earth Summit), held in June in Rio de Janeiro, provided explosive material for the conservative groups. They took the opportunity to brandish their old arguments against defining the limits of indigenous territories, alleging the hypothetical danger of the "internationalization" of Amazonia. In so doing, they masked the presence of multinationals, the subordination of national economic policy to the interests of the International Monetary Fund and other international creditors, and the privatization program, all of which were much more serious indicators of the internationalization of all of the country's wealth.

In the second week of June, during ECO-92, an important event occurred, with both national and international implications: publication by the weekly magazine *Veja* of a report on the presumed rape of a student from the town of Redençao, in the State of Para, which the Kayapo Indian leader Paulinho Paiakan was accused of committing.

This biased version of events caused profound consternation throughout Brazil and produced a negative impact which fostered the growth of discrimination in all its forms and the manifestation of prejudices which still persist today.

We are convinced that these reports were another coup by the anti-indigenous forces, seeking to undermine the social base of the Indian cause, since the Indian image from then on was associated with marginal elements and urban violence.

However, ECO-92 was the determining factor in the Indian declaration of occupation of their territories. President Collor de Mello feared that his international image would be compromised by disclosure of his government's failure to respect its constitutional commitments to the indigenous peoples and the environment. In reality, Collor de Mello's actions were intended only as a marketing strategy. Apart from what his Minister of Justice had done, nothing had been accomplished to promote the physical delimitation of these territories or guarantee assistance to education, health and production. Very few declarations of occupation of Indian territories were made, few budget resources were allocated for this purpose and few administrative actions were undertaken by FUNAI to assist and protect indigenous communities.

It nevertheless must be acknowledged that the new President of FUNAI, Sidney Possuelo,[15] embarked on the process of defining Indian territories and showed greater openness towards Indian and pro-Indian representatives.

In June 1992, another blow was struck against the physical delimitation of Indian territories. The Union Court of Accounts approved a document by Minister Fernando Gonçalves, reporting on the audit conducted at IBAMA. On that occasion, it expressed its perplexity about the "fact that the process of creating conservation units and indigenous reserves has occurred without a larger debate, especially with technical agencies such as the National Department of Mine Production, ELECTROBRAS [the Brazilian electrical power company] and EMBRAPA, as well as the agency responsible for questions of national security, the EMA [Army General Staff], organizations capable of evaluating the mineral and energy potential and the strategic interest of these regions."

As a result, three months later, the anti-indigenous forces persuaded the President of the Republic to decide illegally, in Notice No. 745 of the Presidency's General Secretariat, that effective July 15, 1992, the comments by Minister Fernando Gonçalves of the Court of Accounts would be adopted in administrative practice.

The impeachment of Collor de Mello in December 1992 brought Itamar Franco to the Presidency of the Republic. He intended to build his government with the help of a broad coalition of political forces which would give him the support of the Congress.

In the area of indigenous policy, the Franco government was content to keep Sidney Possuelo as President of FUNAI. On indigenous issues, Franco's Minister of Justice, Senator Mauricio Corréa, displayed a vacillating attitude in the defence of Indian rights, as was shown in the cases of Irai and Cachoeira Seca. In these two cases, after legally defining the limits of the territories traditionally occupied by the Kaingangs and the Araras respectively, the Minister gave in to pressure from local political and economic interests and put these limits into question. Fortunately, this change was not concretized, because of the very hostile public reaction to the decision. Fearing the erosion of his image in Congress, the media and the government, the Minister reconfirmed his earlier decisions.

Concerned about possible reversals by the new government on indigenous policy due to the greater influence of nationalist forces, CIMI alerted the leadership of the Co-ordinating Council of Indigenous Peoples and Organizations to the importance of stepping up political contacts with Congress and the executive branch.

A committee of this Council visited Brasilia in October 1992 and established good contacts with the Nationalist Congressional Front. It also obtained audiences with the Ministers of Justice and the Marine and with the Army General Staff.

Later on, in November 1992, CIMI established new contacts with progressive and left-wing elected representatives from the Workers Party (PT) and the Brazilian Socialist Party (PSB), especially Hélio Bicudo and Miguel Arraes. They confirmed CIMI's concerns about military pressure and the pseudo-nationalist position of conservatives defending anti-indigenous arguments. Despite a one-year delay, these contacts confirmed the necessity of consolidating congressional support for the indigenous cause, in order to create political conditions favourable to the adoption of administrative measures respectful of Indian peoples.

Action by pro-Indian movements

To have a clear understanding of the nature of this action, we must go back to the resumption of legislative work in early February 1992. At that time, the Special Committee created to study the bills concerning Indians met and decided to begin its deliberations in March, with a presentation followed by discussions with representatives of the different groups which had drafted these bills.

CIMI, which wanted the Committee to consider the bill it had prepared in concert with several indigenous leaders and organizations, presented it under the name of the Indigenous Peoples Law, with the support of elected representatives from several political parties.

In reality, since March 1991, CIMI had been in discussion with its members and with indigenous leaders and communities on a set of proposals likely to produce good and just regulations on constitutional rights, in accordance with the interests of the indigenous peoples. Its other aim was to oppose what the federal government was presenting.

Other non-governmental pro-indigenous groups, who were aware of the same danger, had also begun to draft another bill under NDI's co-ordination.

From March to May 1992, the Committee discussed a number of themes, but soon interrupted this work, partially because the majority of its members were not interested.

However, the "Indians of Brazil" Committee organized by the City of Sao Paulo Secretariat of Culture took the initiative of inviting CIMI, NDI and FUNAI representatives to debate their proposed indigenous legislation.

After two meetings in May and June, CIMI, the NDI and FUNAI, with the participation of the federal Public Ministry, discussed the content of the bills in order to reach a consensus on some issues and present common amendments to the proposals of the Special

Committee's reporter, which they already knew would be very negative.

On December 3, 1992, Congresswoman Teresa Jucá won election as Mayor of Boa Vista. With the consent of the President of the Special Committee, a meeting was organized to study Teresa Jucá's work before she left Congress. The main issues, such as defining the limits of indigenous territories, exploitation of mineral deposits and other questions, received very negative treatment in her report.

At this point, it was already known that the results of this work depended on the follow-up done by the Committee's new reporter and the position of the anti-indigenous elected representatives. Taking advantage of Jucá's departure, the pro-indigenous members of the Committee took steps to choose a new reporter with less anti-indigenous positions.

At the beginning of the legislative year 1993, the Congressman from Parana, Luciano Pizzato, of the *Partido da Frente Liberal* (PFL-PR), was elected as the Committee's reporter. He had not yet taken a position on the merits of the proposed legislation, nor had he put forward other proposals.

However, around mid-June 1993, faced with the possibility that the new reporter would take a stand, CIMI, NDI and the Public Ministry held another meeting. They went further in their quest for a consensus, particularly on the articles dealing with mining, definition of territorial limits and elimination of the partial incapacity and trusteeship to which the Indians were subject. They also defined clearer and more efficient mechanisms for protection of the material and cultural property of the indigenous peoples.

Pressure was now exerted on elected representatives interested in the indigenous question so that common proposals could be transmitted officially to the reporter of the Special Committee.

The indigenous peoples and their organizations were contacted, especially by CIMI, to inform them of these discussions. However, a mechanism still had to be created for the entire Indian and pro-Indian movement to make its positions known.

Efforts were made in this sense. In addition to meetings in the villages and on the reserves, a new meeting took place in April 1992, bringing together representatives of 101 peoples, 55 indigenous organizations and 350 leaders. They analyzed the three bills under discussion and took a position on each of the issues treated.

Comparison of the proposed legislation

The bills on Indians, indigenous peoples and indigenous societies, submitted by the government, CIMI and NDI respectively, concern the relations between Indian peoples and their communities, on the one hand, and the State and non-indigenous societies, on the other. Each bill is based on a distinct concept. Here, with comments and comparisons, are a few of the issues covered in the three bills.

Responsibilities of the central governments, States and municipalities

The responsibilities of the Union, the States and the municipalities are discussed in the first part of each bill.

CIMI assigns the following duties to the Federal Union:

a) physical delimitation of the traditional territories occupied by Indians;

b) protection of indigenous property;

c) ensuring assistance as provided by law.

For States, municipalities and the Federal District, CIMI proposes that each create its own mechanisms or agencies to ensure that everybody respects indigenous property and ethnic and cultural diversity.

NDI affirms that it is up to the Union to protect and promote the indigenous rights defined in the Constitution and regulated by law. It also proposes that the preparation and implementation of national defence plans, territorial organization and economic development at the national and regional levels not injure indigenous rights.

This rule is completely useless. Not only must the preparation and implementation of the three plans set out in Article 1, paragraph 3 of this bill not injure indigenous rights, but according to the Constitution, the constitutional validity of any other action, regardless of its nature, depends on its respect for indigenous property.

However, it is the government bill which offers the most problematical formulation. It approaches the responsibilities of administrative units from the perspective of a policy of protection and assistance to Indians and indigenous communities. This policy would be implemented via a set of government actions co-ordinated by the Union through a federal Indian assistance agency.

With the exception of this policy, the Union would rely on the participation of States and municipalities, within the limits of their jurisdiction, and on the co-operation of public and private agencies.

The government's idea that the Union should co-ordinate government actions, with the participation of States and municipalities, is contrary to the constitutional provision whereby it is up to the Union alone to ensure physical delimitation of territories traditionally occupied by Indians and protect and enforce respect for their property. This proposal would weaken the power of the Union by sharing it with the States and municipalities, thus opening the door to regionalization of indigenous policy.

This proposal seeks the participation not only of pro-indigenous groups but also of employers and associations of big landowners and forest or mining companies. This seems out of place and unacceptable, because these are the parties that do the most harm to indigenous peoples.

Definitions of the subject of the legislation

In defining the subjects of the indigenous legislation, there are important similarities and differences between the three bills. Each defines the subject of the legislation in different terms:

a) "indigenous people" for CIMI;
b) "indigenous community" for the government;
c) "indigenous society" for NDI.

An indigenous people is made up of those who organize themselves socially, politically and culturally in their own way, differentiated by ethnic specificity within the Brazilian State, and maintaining historical links with pre-Columbian societies.

Indigenous communities are human groups with social, cultural or economic characteristics distinct from those of the society around them, and whose members identify themselves and are identified as pre-Columbian societies.

Indigenous societies are socially organized groups, made up of one or more communities, which consider themselves distinct from the society around them and maintain historical links with pre-Columbian societies.

CIMI and NDI accept the possibility that the people or society may be made up of more than one community, thereby recognizing the fact that ethnic groups are subdivided into sub-groups with identical ethnic and cultural characteristics, an aspect which should not be disregarded. This vision represents progress in understanding Brazil's pluriethnic reality.

However, the points of view of the government and NDI are distinct from that of CIMI, because they define indigenous identity not in terms of itself but in relation to the majority Brazilian society.

The Indian registry

NDI proposes that the birth and death registries of the Indians, kept by FUNAI, have the same legal value as the notarial registry required for all citizens.

This proposal confers the responsibility on FUNAI to organize the registries, which are subject to judicial authority.

Yet Article 236 of the federal Constitution stipulates that notarial and registration services will be provided by private firms delegated by the State. The NDI proposal therefore runs up against a constitutional impediment.

CIMI and the government approach this question identically. Both consider that the registry must follow the rules of the common legislation. CIMI, however, aims beyond births and deaths to civil identification, meaning identity papers. The government, on the contrary, does not take account of this type of registry which is not produced by a notary, but by the State's public security bureaus.

This measure is of great practical importance, because it establishes proof of the ethnic identity of the person bearing the card. In addition to this difference, it is also noted that, unlike the government, CIMI does not demand control of the marriage registry. In this, NDI's position is close to that of CIMI since it considers that the internal relations of an indigenous society, such as marriage, must be regulated according to its usages, customs and traditions.

CIMI and NDI have an identical understanding of the legal nature of the subjects of their bills. These are indigenous peoples and communities for CIMI and indigenous societies for NDI. Their bills suggest the inclusion of a standard of interpretation of this question, given that they recognize that indigenous communities, peoples and societies have a specific legal personality in domestic public law and do not owe their existence to a registry.

Indigenous heritage

This chapter lists the property which constitutes the heritage of indigenous peoples. This subject is important because of the constitutional provision on protection of property by the Union and respect for this property by everyone.

a) Indigenous property

CIMI and the government define indigenous property in a very similar manner. They propose that it include both material property and property of a cultural nature. Material property includes the right to the land and to possession and enjoyment of the communities' natural wealth and acquisitions. Cultural property would result from the manifestation of each people's culture. The two proposals are innovative compared to the existing legislation.

NDI approaches this theme in a very special way. Its bill does not identify indigenous property but is only concerned with its administration and with royalties and copyright. It also only deals with intellectual property, distinguishing between those who can obtain a patent and those who cannot.

Patents could be obtained for inventions, models or projects resulting from indigenous knowledge.

In reality, this possibility has always existed to the extent that the Industrial Property Law was applied adequately to Brazil's pluriethnic reality.

As for intellectual property which cannot be patented, NDI proposes that it be protected. It defines this property as "any and all useful knowledge, especially on pharmaceutical products and natural species known to Indians, for which industrial and commercial applications and uses can be found." NDI also suggests that this knowledge can be used by others in exchange for compensation.

This indicates the appetite of major multinational economic interests for the indigenous peoples' knowledge of the biological diversity of the territories they occupy. This diversity represents a great source of wealth coveted by various interests. This subject should be approached with caution.

b) Ownership of indigenous property

The three proposals consider that the owner of indigenous property is the indigenous community which occupies the territory.

c) Administration of indigenous property

Management or administration of this property is also recognized by all proposals as belonging to the indigenous community. However, NDI accepts that the community ask the Federal Union to handle some of this property.

CIMI, on the other hand, proposes that property or royalties belonging to or intended for Indians be administered by the Federal Union as long as their rightful owners, all the indigenous peoples of Brazil, have not decided how to administer them.

d) Exclusive use of territories

CIMI, concerned about the importance and implications of this subject, proposes that an interpretative rule be included in the law regarding the exercise of the right to exclusive use of the wealth of the land, rivers and lakes of territories traditionally occupied by the Indians.

What is new is the statement that the Indians' exclusive use of their natural wealth must not compromise the future use of their resources.

The indigenous peoples and communities hold the inherent rights to ownership of the territory they traditionally occupy, even if it is registered in the name of the Federal Union.

Legal relations

The important question raised here is how to protect and enforce respect for indigenous property in the relations that communities and Indians will establish with non-Indians, and how to proceed in these relations. The term "non-Indians" means natural or legal persons, whether Brazilian or foreign.

The three bills coincide in suggesting that internal relations or dealings between Indians or between indigenous communities should be settled according to the usages, customs and traditions of the communities.

However, the three bills differ on the rules they present for relations between Indians and non-Indians.

CIMI presumes that Indians have the full capacity to exercise their rights and are not subject to any trusteeship or assistance.

Taking into account the constitutional provision on respect for indigenous property, CIMI declares that any act which injures them must be nullified, because it would not respect indigenous property.

The clause stipulating that indigenous property must be respected in all cases is intended to guarantee a balance in relations where both parties have obligations and rights. This is required because of the ethnic and cultural diversity of indigenous peoples and communities.

The Indians' ignorance and incomprehension of the rules governing legal and economic relations in Brazilian society must be considered and respected, because they are due to cultural differences.

Not only Indians must understand and know the workings of Brazilian society to be on a level playing field with that society. Non-Indians have the same obligations to indigenous people.

When acts dictated by ignorance of a people's culture and lifestyle harm the indigenous heritage, they must not be considered valid. When a community or an Indian suffers such prejudice, the federal Public Ministry, or even the indigenous organization to which the community is affiliated, may ask the federal court to annul the act and set the necessary damages.

NDI considers that acts or legal transactions which harm indigenous people or the indigenous community or society and which affect the community's property are null and void. NDI thus limits the nullity of acts to those which affect indigenous heritage property.

CIMI's proposal is broader in that it proposes the nullity of any act which harms indigenous property.

Unlike CIMI, NDI proposes that part of the compensation be assumed by the Federal Union, meaning that the Union would pay the indemnity and then obtain reimbursement from the responsible party. The other part of the reparations, the lost income of the Indian community or individual, would be the responsibility of the community, the individual or the federal Public Ministry.

Making the Union responsible for compensation owed by a third party opens the door to reproduction of paternalistic practices frequently condemned by several pro-indigenous sectors and by countless indigenous leaders. Such responsibility also has the disadvantage of making it possible for the government to interfere in the community's internal affairs.

The NDI's bill seems to want to end trusteeship, but it allows the maintenance of a new form of State interference in the relations between the Indians and national society. With such a rule, it is natural and even necessary that the public administration intervene in contracts or agreements signed between Indian communities and non-Indians, because if any damages are caused to Indians as a result, the government will have to dip into the tax base of the entire population to pay compensation.

The government bill maintains the current system of trusteeship exercised by the Union through a "federal Indian assistance agency." It assumes that Indians are incapable of establishing relations with Brazilian society, as a result of their relative civil incapacity, since they neither know nor understand its values or its workings.

The government's proposal, which sets out requirements for ending trusteeship established by judicial decision, establishes the following conditions: minimum age of 21; knowledge of the Portuguese language, and understanding of the dominant usages and customs in Brazilian society, confirmed by FUNAI's expert opinion. Full capacity for the exercise of civil and political rights would thus be diminished.

As stated earlier, the Federal Constitution eliminated this outlook when it adopted the principle of respect for ethnic and cultural diversity.

It is disturbing to see that the government bill considers that Indians do not have the full capacity to exercise their political rights. This means that they are not full citizens. What part of their citizenship would be taken away? Could they vote but not be elected? Or could they vote and be elected with FUNAI's assistance? Whatever the chosen solution, this is unacceptable immorality and an unconstitutional aim.

It is also disturbing to note, in this same proposal, that the end of trusteeship is only foreseen for Indians as individuals, and that their communities would remain permanently subject to it.

Regarding the exercise of trusteeship, the government bill barely differs from the current situation.

The most important difference concerns FUNAI's obligation to assist in transactions of a legal nature. If it does not do so, the transaction may be nullified when its object is:

a) land collectively owned by Indians;
b) rights to the community's technology and inventions.

Strangely, the trustee's assistance is also required in the case of real estate transactions involving Indian individuals.

The government bill also considers transactions are null and void if they are made in bad faith and cause prejudice to the heritage of the community or of Indians as individuals.

This bill is therefore unacceptable, since it is based on outmoded parameters.

Relations with public authorities

The bills deal with six aspects of relations with executive and judicial authorities.

a) Policing power

According to the government and NDI, the policing power must be exercised only by the Union in indigenous territories, through the Indian assistance agency.

According to CIMI, it is up to the federal public administration to exercise the policing power with the participation of the indigenous communities. CIMI also suggests that the right of communities to protect their own property be standardized.

CIMI's proposal provides that policing can be done from outside a reserve if this is the community's wish. In this way, for example, some indigenous communities may opt to have the indigenous assistance stations located outside the territories they occupy.

The federal public administration, the federal police or any other central government authority could have access to indigenous territories in the exercise of duties prescribed by law. CIMI proposes that these activities be carried out with the community to guarantee respect for its social organization and the indigenous people's authority over its territory.

b) Access and residence in indigenous territory

On the issue of access and residence of outsiders in the territories, the three bills give the indigenous communities the power of authorization. However, the government makes access and residence conditional on adherence to criteria established by FUNAI, while NDI expressly prohibits this possibility. Even if the requirement of health certificates and prior identification of individuals may be considered objective criteria, this possibility must be analyzed in the light of administrative reality, where abuses are frequent. For example, several presidents of FUNAI claimed to have the power to decide who could or could not enter indigenous territory.

c) Prohibition of access to indigenous territories

The government and NDI foresee the possibility of provisionally prohibiting access to indigenous territories without physical boundaries, so as to ensure the physical and cultural integrity of Indians and their communities.

CIMI does not propose this measure because it believes it to be useless. The policing power should be exercised over Indians and indigenous property regardless of whether the territories have physical boundaries.

Prohibition, as a provisional measure until territorial limits are set, may be a useful administrative instrument, but it does not replace the importance and necessity of physical delimitation.

d) Police and army participation

For the exercise of the policing power, the bills provide for federal police participation. The government and NDI conceive this participation as co-operation with the Public Ministry, the communities and FUNAI. CIMI sees the role of the federal police as an obligation to provide police support to the Public Ministry, the communities, their organizations and FUNAI.

CIMI accepts that the army can intervene to protect indigenous property, according to the conditions set out in Article 142 of the Constitution. This rule is useless, given the constitutional provisions. NDI provides that the army may be called in at the request of the Public Ministry, indigenous societies and FUNAI. There is no constitutional foundation to allow this.

NDI proposes the collaboration of auxiliary forces, namely the military police. CIMI excludes this possibility because of the serious problems already caused by this police force in conflicts with indigenous peoples. The government does not specifically provide for the collaboration of the military police, but according to the rule's application and in accepting the participation of States in the Indian protection and assistance policy (Article 2), military police intervention could be requested.

e) Legal capacity

CIMI consolidates two constitutional provisions in the same article: the provision which includes the judicial defence of indigenous rights and interests among the functions of the Public Ministry and the provision which gives Indians, their communities and their organizations the legal capacity to appear in court.

The government makes the same proposal as CIMI, but adds that FUNAI is also a legitimate party.

NDI copies Article 232 of the federal Constitution. It does not matter that the formulation does not mention the Public Ministry, since the text of the Constitution takes precedence over ordinary laws.

f) Jurisdiction of federal justice

The jurisdiction of the federal justice system is an important aspect of the relationship with judicial authority, since it allows Indians to be subpoenaed and judged. CIMI and NDI want this jurisdiction to be federal, but the government's bill gives it to the States.

There are two fundamental reasons to give the federal justice system jurisdiction over criminal matters concerning Indians.

Firstly, the federal Constitution has expressly assigned the federal executive branch the responsibility for delimitation of indigenous lands and for protecting and enforcing respect for indigenous property. It has assigned the federal legislative branch the exclusive responsibility for legislating on indigenous populations, and for authorizing exploration and development of water resources and prospecting and exploitation of mineral wealth. It has given the federal judicial branch jurisdiction over disputes relating to indigenous rights. The text of the Constitution entrusts the federal government with administrative, legislative and judicial actions concerning Indians.

The Constitution also gives federal justice the jurisdiction to judge penal offenses which affect the Union's property, services and interests (Article 109-IV) and determines its responsibility in protecting and enforcing respect for indigenous property and the physical delimitation of territories occupied by the Indians (Article 231).

It is clear that the Federal Union has the duty to protect the Indians and their property. This has repercussions for federal jurisdiction, as Articles 109-IV and 231 of the Constitution attest.

Physical delimitation of territories

Each bill proposes a different procedure for the physical delimitation of the boundaries of indigenous territories.

The government's bill maintains the conception of Article 19 of the 1973 Indian Status Act with the following changes:

1. It gives FUNAI the power to co-ordinate the administrative delimitation, while removing its authoritative power. This means that the designation and delimitation must be approved by other government agencies.

2. It recognizes FUNAI's jurisdiction to issue a notice declaring occupation within 30 days after the conclusion of technical studies of the boundaries. This notice will be the basis for physical delimitation.

3. It also establishes a one-year deadline from the beginning of the physical delimitation procedure for the President of the Republic to conclude it by homologation.

4. It provides that the homologation registry be kept at the Union Heritage Department and that notice be given to the land registry office of the administrative division where the territories are located.

5. It considers the homologation transcript of territories traditionally occupied by Indians and their reserved territories as title of ownership.

6. Contrary to the Indian Law currently in force, Article 38 of the government's bill gives invaders of indigenous territories a legal argument allowing them to prevent delimitation.

7. The limits of the indigenous territories may be redefined when they are considered to be insufficient for the physical and cultural survival of the indigenous groups.

The CIMI and NDI bills, unlike that of the government, suggest that the law define how the Union will carry out the physical delimitation of indigenous territories. NDI considers that Indian territories are already delimited if they were recognized by FUNAI or by the competent federal authority before the new law came into force. It sets a 60-day deadline for the President of FUNAI to publish the list of all recognized indigenous territories in the official gazette, the *Diario Oficial da Uniao.*

This proposal is potentially dangerous for indigenous peoples and thus for the federal public heritage. Many administrative dossiers concerning the delimitation of territories do not consider the exact dimensions of the lands occupied by indigenous peoples, is either because the dossiers were poorly constituted or because they were opened in a legal context predating the new Constitution, which meant that they did not consider the definition of "lands traditionally occupied" by Indians, as stated in Article 23 of the new federal Constitution.

In several cases, more than one delimitation exists for the same indigenous territories.

The NDI bill provides that the delimitation procedure may be administrative or judicial.

The judicial procedure provided in the NDI bill has one peculiarity: it harms indigenous rights when it deals with immovable property located, at least in part, in the region to be delimited. Judicial delimitation of an indigenous territory, as defined by NDI, allows participation in this operation by persons interested in the occupation of these territories, namely potential invaders.

If two landowners go to court to dispute the possession of land considered, at least in part, to be territory traditionally occupied by Indians, it would be natural, especially if the Brazilian legislation is taken into account, for these two landowners to resort to the judicial demarcation procedure to prove, not separately but jointly, that the land in question was not traditionally occupied by Indians.

According to CIMI, the federal public administration would be responsible, with the indigenous community, for delimitation of territories traditionally occupied by this community.

This step is the decisive point at which to determine the limits of the territory traditionally occupied by an indigenous people.

After all the elements which prove traditional occupation are assembled, the limits would be submitted for community approval.

Once the community has given its consent, FUNAI would implement the administrative procedure, including physical delimitation and registration with the Union Heritage Department.

CIMI's proposal, in addition to the administrative procedure for territorial delimitation, would guarantee communities the right to promote this delimitation. However, they must possess the elements which prove their traditional occupation, the map and the description of the limits.

These documents would be submitted to FUNAI. After verifying compliance with paragraph 1 of Article 231, FUNAI would homologate the delimitation, determine the placement of official boundary markers and make the necessary registrations.

If FUNAI disagreed with the limits established by the community or by the indigenous people, it then would have to proceed with administrative delimitation.

CIMI's proposal, therefore, gives priority to participation by the indigenous community, though it emphasizes the importance of proving traditional occupation with appropriate documents.

Prospecting and mining

The federal Constitution grants special treatment to mining in indigenous territory.

Paragraph 1 of Article 176 determines that prospecting and mining will be done in accordance with the national interest, by Brazilians or Brazilian companies, under the conditions provided by law.

The following questions are raised by the constitutional text:

1. How will the National Congress authorize prospecting and mining in indigenous territory?
2. How will the indigenous peoples be consulted?
3. What specific conditions will be necessary for prospecting and mining in indigenous territory?

The government's bill sets the following two conditions to assess the request for a prospecting and mining authorization: verification of the insufficiency, in relation to the country's needs, of known reserves of the ore that the applicant wishes to prospect or mine, and the fact that the indigenous territories have been delimited, without conflict or invasion, or that they are not occupied by Indian peoples who are unknown or with no contact with national society.

Moreover, according to the government's bill, Congress may consult the federal agencies responsible for the environment, indigenous assistance and mines. It is useless to provide for this possibility when it is up to the legislative branch to request the information it deems necessary.

Finally, the government's bill renders prospecting and mining subject to the existence of a contract, signed with FUNAI's assistance, between the authorized person and the community which occupies the territory where the prospecting or mining will take place. This will be done in order to define, among other conditions, the percentage of the community's share in the proceeds, which may not be less than 10 percent of the ore's total value.

The NDI bill considers the mineral resources of the indigenous territories as national reserves, which may be prospected and mined according to the proposed procedure.

Before dealing with the procedure necessary for prospecting and mining of ore in indigenous territories, the bill provides that the Federal Union will conduct a geological study in the territories traditionally occupied by Indians in order to determine their mineral potential.

The information thus obtained would allow verification of the first requirement of the bill. NDI poses the same preconditions as the government regarding congressional study of the request.

Once mining has been authorized, the President of the Republic would issue a "mining decree" which would subordinate mining to a written contract between the company and the indigenous community, assisted by the federal Public Ministry. The contract should specify:

a) the community's percentage interest in the proceeds of the mining operation, which would not be less than 5 percent of the monetary value of the ore extracted; and b) the possibility for the indigenous community to oversee the work of the mining company.

Finally, the bill accepts that Congress could suspend or end the prospecting or mining authorization at any time, if the conditions established by law are not respected or for other reasons of a legal nature.

The coup of constitutional revision

While these bills were under study, the majority of the National Congress approved the idea of a revision of the Constitution. This decision was motivated politically by the fact that foreign companies and the IMF wanted Brazil to remove all barriers from its Constitution to foreign investment in the exploitation of the country's wealth.

The federal government also wanted fiscal reform and strongly favoured revision.

However, many individuals and organizations spoke out against this constitutional revision, which was directed against the gains of 1988. Among them were progressive and leftist political parties, jurists, democratic and liberal elected representatives, the Brazilian Order of Lawyers, the Brazilian Press Association, the Brazilian National Conference of Bishops, the One Workers Central, the General Confederation of Workers, the National Student Union, the Landless Rural Workers Movement and dozens of others.

For the indigenous peoples, and for the Brazilian people, this revision of the Constitution represents a major risk that the guarantees in force since October 5, 1988 will be rolled back. During these five years, the dominant groups opposed to the rights of indigenous peoples used the newspapers and Congress to spread the false idea that the Indians would have exaggerated privileges that had to be revised.

Due to this new political and institutional situation, some groups claim that the congressional discussion on the new legislation on indigenous peoples should be suspended, in case Congress revised the Constitution and rolled back indigenous rights.

The dominant elites wanted the revision of the Constitution to be completed no later than the first three months of 1994.

The democratic, progressive and popular forces first want to discuss the internal rules of Congress, the current version of which impedes effective participation by the congressional minority in constitutional revision.

The Federal Supreme Court is also analyzing several complaints of unconstitutionality filed against the constitutional revision.

In addition to this political agitation, there are the tensions produced by the grave political crisis in Congress triggered by corruption charges against elected representatives responsible for preparing the Union budget.

The credibility of several members of Congress was deeply shaken. Several political groups and some members of the press therefore maintain that the constitutional revision is not viable and are demanding early general elections.

With regard to the interests of the indigenous peoples, we believe that the Special Committee of the House of Representatives should continue to analyze the bills, discuss a new Indian Law as soon as possible and submit it to the Federal Senate for approval.

To obtain this, we are counting on mobilization by the Indians, pressure from their allies in Brazil and the inestimable power of international solidarity.

Notes

1. The term "Indian," employed as a noun or as an adjective, is used in Brazil with no pejorative connotation. We therefore have chosen to retain it rather than always replacing it with the word "indigenous."

2. Beatriz Perrone-Moisés, of the Sao Paulo University Centre for Research in Indian History and Indigenism. Ms. Perrone-Moisés, an anthropologist, contributed to a collective work on the history of Brazilian Indians, *Historia dos Indios no Brasil*, edited by Manuela Carneiro da Cunha, published in 1992.

3. In 1990, 48 percent of Brazil's indigenous population lived in the Northern Amazon region.

4. In the past few years, signs have been found in Amazonia of the presence of 53 groups which still have no contact with national society. The existence of 12 of these groups has already been confirmed by the National Indian Foundation, FUNAI (see CEDI 1993).

5. Among these development megaprojects in Amazonia, we should note the Trans-Amazonian, Northern Perimeter and other highways, the Tucurui hydroelectric complex, the Carajas Iron Project and the Calha Norte project. For detailed analyses of the impact of some of these projects on the Indians of Amazonia, see: Leinad A. Santos and Lucia M. M. de Andrade, *Hydroelectric Dams on Brazil's Xinga River and Indigenous Peoples*, Cambridge, Cultural Survival/Pro-Indian Commission of Sao Paulo, 1990, (*Cultural Survival Report* no 30); and articles on the hydroelectric complexes, the agro-industrial megaprojects, forest exploitation, development and geopolitics in Bruce Albert, "Brésil, Indiens et développement en Amazonie," *Ethnies*, 11-12, spring 1990, (Survival International-France). This important dossier, which contains articles on several aspects of the Indian question in Brazil, also has a fairly complete bibliography.

6. Manuela Carneiro da Cunha, "Criterios de indianidade ou liçaes de antropofagia," *Folha de São Paulo*, 12/01/81 (translated into English in *Survival International Review*, Vol. 6, nos 5-6, 1982); and Eduardo Viveiros de Castro, "Debate," in H. Saboya (ed.), *O Indio e o Direito*, Rio de Janeiro, OAB/RJ, 1981, pp. 63-75.

7. Manuela Carneiro da Cunha, (ed.), *Os Direitos do Indio. Ensaios e documentos*. Sao Paulo, Ed. Brasilense, 1987.

8. The laws provided for exploitation by public or private mining companies. This type of invasion of Indian territories, as well as the invasion by thousands of gold prospectors (*garimpeiros*), was one of the major causes of destruction of Indian lands and populations in recent decades. The recent case of the Yanomamis, whose lands were invaded several times, is a tragic example. See the articles on the mining question in Bruce Albert, op. cit.

9. Regarding the battles waged in the Constituent Assembly of 1987 on the Indian question, see the article by M. Carneiro da Cunha in Bruce Albert, op. cit.

10. A translation of the articles of the Constitution relating to the rights of Indian peoples can be found in Appendix IX.

11. See Bruce Albert, op. cit., p. 3.

12. The demarcation deadlines had already passed in 1978. In 1973, the Indian Status Law required that demarcation of all Indian territories in Brazil be concluded within five years; in 1984, out of 67 million hectares concerned, only 3% were already delimited and homologated, 19% were delimited but not homologated and 78% were simply recognized (see Carneiro da Cunha, op. cit., p. 35).

13. Paulo Machado Guimaraes is a lawyer with CIMI, an organization which has played a very active part in the reform of the Constitution. CIMI is an NGO which supports the indigenous communities through different programs and services.

14. NDI is a pro-indigenous NGO which provides legal assistance to indigenous communities (ed. note).

15. Since the writing of this article in October 1993, Sidney Possuelo has been relieved of his position and this agency has reverted to its usual anti-indigenous style (ed. note).

Postscript

by Marie Léger

After a long struggle to obtain international recognition, the indigenous peoples have finally shattered the wall of silence which isolated them for 500 years. The last decade of this century is likely to be full of changes.

Marginalized by a system which had excluded them from the wave of decolonization, the indigenous peoples are on the road to recognition of their collective existence and their right to enjoy the powers granted to other peoples of the world. Will this new presence bring about a redefinition of Nation-States, the current subjects of international law? Unlike the earlier decolonization, this one does not seek to multiply the number of independent States, but to force existing States to welcome diversity. The quest for indigenous sovereignty is not secessionist.

Everywhere in the Americas, as the essays in this collection show, people are seeking recognition for cultural pluralism within States that they hope to make plurinational. The assimilator-integrator model which claimed to make all individuals equal and similar subjects is being called into question. It is now necessary to find equality through respect for collective differences and autonomy.

International standards are evolving rapidly. Convention 169 of the International Labour Organization already seeks to protect collective cultural integrity in terms of linguistic, judicial, territorial and other practices. The future Universal Declaration will make the indigenous peoples full collective subjects and overturn the legal and political conceptions concerning them. However, there is a gap, and sometimes a gulf, between discourse and reality which can only be bridged with time and considerable effort.

A few Latin American constitutions deal with indigenous rights. There is no model to follow or example to reproduce in this matter. Each case reflects a particular history and geography. It is also the result of pressure from organized movements, sometimes after wars or revolts. However, there are some elements on which we can reflect.

The Nicaraguan Constitution opts for a regional and multiethnic approach. Although it recognizes the indigenous languages as official in the territory in which they are used, as well as the traditional tenure of communal lands, autonomy is reserved for the regions. It is the regions which benefit from royalties on natural resources and which enjoy the essential features of administrative autonomy. These regions are multiethnic. Multiethnicity is even a fundamental characteristic of regional institutions. The region is more extensive than an exclusively Amerindian territory would have been. In the Northern region, one quarter of Nicaragua's territory, indigenous people account for nearly half the population and constitute an important political force. They nevertheless must create a common practice with the territory's other populations, a concerted way of looking at the future and development.

Despite the narrow limits of the constitutional text, Panamanian laws opt for an approach completely different from that of the Nicaraguan Constitution. For the Kunas, it is possible to speak of an ethnic territory and government, which allows the coexistence of institutions of very different natures. The Kuna General Congress does not function on the same principles as Panamanian institutions. Recognition of an exclusive territory for the Kunas makes it possible to establish a special connection with resources and the environment. The explicit recognition of institutions unique to the Kunas and of their jurisdiction in controlling the development of their portion of the territory is an original feature. However, the area involved is limited.

The new Colombian Constitution adopts an ethnic approach while facilitating participation in national political life. It recognizes that ethnic diversity is a fundamental component of the nation. It recognizes the official status of indigenous languages in the territories where they are spoken. Indigenous territories managed by territorial councils are instituted. Though they do not have exclusive powers, the councils have a role to play in questions relating to land use, settlement of territories, public investments, fiscal and natural resources, programs intended for communities inhabiting the territories, public order and representation to the government.

In Nicaragua, Panama and Colombia, indigenous people are represented in the democratic institutions of their respective countries. Their affiliation to these States is not called into question. In Colombia, the indigenous movement not only defends its participation in national political life but claims to offer solutions that respond to the concerns and aspirations of a majority of citizens. It takes positions on respect for minorities as well as the decentralization of institutions. It sees itself as a national political player.

The context is different in Brazil. The constitutional reform sought to remove the trusteeship imposed on the indigenous peoples, but the question of the vast indigenous territories and control of their resources is at the centre of tremendous power struggles.

Despite the different forms taken by constitutional approaches, indigenous organizations everywhere have the same difficulty enforcing respect for their legal gains. The lack of political will makes it difficult to apply official texts. In all cases, control of resources and territorial development is the key to controversy. The best preserved forests are the ones most coveted and the ones where indigenous people live.

Recognition of the rights of indigenous peoples will require great political creativity from everyone. Changes both in international standards and in national constitutions are in progress. In the long term, more or less, these changes will imply a new approach to human rights and a transformation of Nation-States. Relying on the wealth of cultural diversity is one way to meet the challenges of development and renewal of political models. To become part of people's everyday reality, autonomy, whatever its form, will always have to confront the powerful financial interests that exploit natural resources.

Convention 169 of the International Labour Organization (ILO)[1]

This Convention was ratified first by Mexico and Norway, then by Colombia, Bolivia, Costa Rica, Paraguay and Peru.

It came into force in September 1991, twelve months after ratification by two members (Mexico and Norway) was registered by the Director General.

A committee of experts analyzes the briefs transmitted each year by the signatory States, reporting on the progress of the Convention's application and the adequacy of national laws to enforce its provisions. In the case of briefs which do not reflect reality or in the case of explicit violations of the Convention's standards, it is possible for indigenous organizations to file complaints with the ILO office in Geneva or ally themselves with workers' representatives who are ILO members.

Excerpts from Convention 169

Preamble

... Recognizing the aspirations of these peoples to exercise control over their own institutions, ways of life and economic development and to maintain and develop their identities, languages and religions, within the framework of the States in which they live; and

Noting that in many parts of the world these peoples are unable to enjoy their fundamental human rights to the same degree as the rest of the population of the States within which they live, and that their laws, values, customs and perspectives have often been eroded; and

Calling attention to the distinctive contributions of indigenous and tribal peoples to the cultural diversity and social and ecological harmony of humankind and to international co-operation and understanding ...

Part I: General Policy

Article 1

1. This Convention applies to:

a) tribal peoples in independent countries whose social, cultural and economic conditions distinguish them from other sections of the national community, and whose status is regulated wholly or partially by their own customs or traditions or by special laws or regulations;

b) peoples in independent countries who are regarded as indigenous on account of their descent from the populations which inhabited the country, or a geographical region to which the country belongs, at the time of conquest or colonization or the establishment of present state boundaries and who, irrespective of their legal status, retain some or all of their own social, economic, cultural and political institutions.

2. Self-identification as indigenous or tribal shall be regarded as a fundamental criterion for determining the groups to which the provisions of this Convention apply.

3. The use of the term "peoples" in this Convention shall not be construed as having any implications as regards the rights which may attach to the term under international law.

Article 3

1. Indigenous and tribal peoples shall enjoy the full measure of human rights and fundamental freedoms without hindrance or discrimination. The provisions of the Convention shall be applied without discrimination to male and female members of these peoples.

Article 5

In applying the provisions of this Convention:

a) the social, cultural, religious and spiritual values and practices of these peoples shall be recognized and protected, and due account shall be taken of the nature of the problems which face them both as groups and as individuals;

b) the integrity of the values, practices and institutions of these peoples shall be respected;

c) policies aimed at mitigating the difficulties experienced by these peoples in facing new conditions of life and work shall be adopted, with the participation and co-operation of the peoples affected.

Article 6

1. In applying the provisions of this Convention, governments shall:

a) consult the peoples concerned, through appropriate procedures and in particular through their representative institutions, whenever consideration is being given to legislative or administrative measures which may affect them directly;

b) establish means by which these peoples can freely participate, to at least the same extent as other sectors of the population, at all levels of decision-making in elective institutions and administrative and other bodies responsible for policies and programmes which concern them;

c) establish means for the full development of these peoples' own institutions and initiatives, and in appropriate cases provide the resources necessary for this purpose ...

Article 7

1. The peoples concerned shall have the right to decide their own priorities for the process of development as it affects their lives, beliefs, institutions and spiritual well-being and the lands they occupy or otherwise use, and to exercise control, to the extent possible, over their own economic, social and cultural development. In addition, they shall participate in the formulation, implementation and evaluation of plans and programmes for national and regional development which may affect them directly ...

Article 9

1. To the extent compatible with the national legal system and internationally recognized rights, the methods customarily practised by the peoples concerned for dealing with offences committed by their members shall be respected.

2. The customs of these peoples in regard to penal matters shall be taken into consideration by the authorities and courts dealing with such cases.

Article 12

The peoples concerned shall be safeguarded against the abuse of their rights and shall be able to take legal proceedings, either individually or through their representative bodies, for the effective protection of these rights. Measures shall be taken to ensure that members of these peoples can understand and be understood in legal proceedings, where necessary through the provision of interpretation or by other effective means.

Part II. Land

Article 14

1. The rights of ownership and possession of the peoples concerned over the lands which they traditionally occupy shall be recognized. In addition, measures shall be taken in appropriate cases to safeguard the right of the peoples concerned to use lands not exclusively occupied by them, but to which they have traditionally had access for their subsistence and traditional activities. Particular attention shall be paid to the situation of nomadic peoples and shifting cultivators in this respect.

2. Governments shall take steps as necessary to identify the lands which the peoples concerned traditionally occupy, and to guarantee effective protection of their rights of ownership and possession.

3. Adequate procedures shall be established within the national legal system to resolve land claims by the peoples concerned.

Article 15

1. The rights of the peoples concerned to the natural resources pertaining to their lands shall be specially safeguarded. These rights include the right of these peoples to participate in the use, management and conservation of these resources.

2. In cases in which the State retains the ownership of mineral or sub-surface resources or rights to other resources pertaining to lands,

governments shall establish or maintain procedures through which they shall consult these peoples, with a view to ascertaining whether and to what degree their interests would be prejudiced, before undertaking or permitting any programmes for the exploration or exploitation of such resources pertaining to their lands. The peoples concerned shall wherever possible participate in the benefits of such activities, and shall receive fair compensation for any changes which they may sustain as a result of such activities.

Part VI. Education and Means of Communication

Article 28

1. Children belonging to the peoples concerned shall, wherever practicable, be taught to read and write in their own indigenous language or in the language most commonly used by the group to which they belong. When this is not practicable, the competent authorities shall undertake consultations with these people with a view to the adoption of measures to achieve this objective ...

Note

1. Agreement concerning indigenous and tribal peoples in independent countries, adopted by the General Conference of the International Labour Organization at its seventy-sixth session, in Geneva, June 27, 1989.

Appendix II
Peoples of the Atlantic Coast of Nicaragua

The Ramas

The Ramas are the least numerous group at present. The Rama population is estimated at about 600 to 700 people, down from at least 1,300 around the year 1700.

They were decimated in the 16th century by Spanish incursions into their ancestral territory, the Rio San Juan region. This is why their language is more closely related to that of the Indians of Costa Rica than to that of the Sumus and Miskitos, although they are all part of the same large Macro Chibcha ethnic family.

The Ramas fled their territory to return to the north in the 18th century because they risked being reduced to slavery, as their river had become a trade route for the Europeans. In fact, once they reached the north, some nevertheless were taken as slaves by the Miskitos.

Few in number, they today are mainly concentrated at Rama Cay. Less than 60 people can still speak their language.[1]

The Garifunas or Black Caribs

The Garifunas are relative newcomers to the region (19th century). Mixed-breed descendants of Caribbean Indians, they are black-skinned but Amerindian by language and culture. Most of those who live in the region left the island of St. Vincent around 1797 after a military defeat. After initially settling in Honduras, they moved south to Nicaragua in search of seasonal employment. Some settled there, while others returned to Honduras in the 1920s. However, the existing Orinoco community probably came directly from St. Vincent. The Garifuna population today is about 1,487.[2]

The Sumus

The name "Sumu" comes from a Miskito word meaning "uncivilized" but designates several distinct communities, including the Ulvas. Like the Ramas, the Sumus were decimated and subjugated by the Miskitos after contact with the Europeans. Many Sumus appear to have been assimilated by the Miskitos and disease, war and slavery all helped to reduce their population. The Sumus live in the Northern Atlantic Region, mainly in scattered inland habitats. Their numbers vary depending on the source: 4,851,[3] 6,000[4] or 13,750.[5] According to Susan Norwood, 9,000 people speak Sumu as their mother tongue.[6]

The Miskitos

Unlike the other indigenous nations, the Miskitos experienced great demographic growth after the European contact and were not numerous in the 17th century. After 1641, interbreeding with Blacks changed their physical appearance. Access to firearms and British political and military support gave them a great strategic advantage over indigenous groups who had less contact with Europeans. This would explain their ability to assimilate some of their neighbours. Around 1700, their influence extended from the Guatemalan border to Panama. However, with the arrival of free Blacks from 1741 to 1860, the Miskitos gradually lost their influence to the benefit of the Creoles. They became increasingly isolated from power and were even victims of discrimination. After 1894, the arrival of the *Mestizos* isolated them even more. The Miskitos found themselves at the bottom of the social ladder. This situation was confirmed under Somoza when the *Mestizos*, in addition to controlling the State apparatus, increasingly gained economic power in the north.

Since 1960, the Miskitos have been geographically divided. Following a decision of the International Court, the northern part of Miskito territory legally became part of Honduras. The Miskitos are of the Moravian religion and not Catholic like most *Mestizos*. The Miskito population varies depending on the source: 66,994,[7] 120,000[8] or 151,250.[9]

The Creoles

The Creoles of the Atlantic Coast are Black, the result of interbreeding between Africans, Amerindians and Europeans. The first Blacks, who were their ancestors, arrived as slaves of the British or as members of buccaneer crews. Some mixed with the Miskitos, while others developed their own culture with a "Creolized" form of English as their mother tongue. In 1770, the population of African origin was estimated at 900 people. Even though the majority were still slaves at that time, Jamaican merchants were settling on the Atlantic Coast and some escaped slaves lived freely.

An elite formed in the 18th and 19th centuries among the merchants and mulattoes freed by their European fathers. They supplanted the Miskitos in the 19th century. After 1894, however, competition developed between Creoles and *Mestizos*. The Creoles predominated among skilled workers, sailors (schooner captains) and professionals. However, most political posts were held by *Mestizos*. Many Creoles belong to the Moravian Church and are concentrated in Bluefields and the surrounding region. Sources estimated their population at between 25,723[10] and 36,000.[11]

The Mestizos

The majority of the people known as *Mestizos* on the Atlantic Coast are *campesinos*, peasant farmers from the Pacific Coast who came to earn a living working for U.S. companies or in Somoza's colonization projects. Others, who are part of the ruling elite, were sent to administer the region.

The first major migrations date from the rubber boom of 1860, which was followed by intensive banana production and mining. In 1927, the Hispanicized *Mestizo* population was estimated at 5,000 individuals. Today, depending on the source, it is estimated at 182,377[12] or 140,000.[13]

Notes

1.   Charles R. Hale and Edmund T. Gordon, "Costeño Demography. Historical and
     Contemporary Demography of Nicaragua's Atlantic Coast," in *Ethnic Groups &
     the Nation-State. The Case of the Atlantic Coast in Nicaragua,* CIDCA and Development Study Unit, University of Stockholm, 1987, pp. 7-32.
2.   Hale and Gordon, op. cit., pp. 21-22.
3.   Hale and Gordon, op. cit.
4.   Hodgson, in *Recherches amérindiennes au Québec,* 1988, Vol.XVIII, no 1, p. 89.
5.   Misurasata, in Hale and Gordon, op. cit., pp. 11-13.
6.   Susan Norwood, in *Wani,* 1987, no 7, p. 41.
7.   Hale and Gordon, op. cit., pp. 15-18.
8.   Hodgson, op. cit.
9.   Misurasata, in Hale and Gordon, op. cit.
10. Hale and Gordon, op. cit., pp. 18-21.
11. Hodgson, op. cit.
12. Hale and Gordon, op. cit., pp. 24-26.
13. Hodgson, op. cit.

Fundamental Principles of the Autonomy Statutes of the Autonomous Regions of Nicaragua's Atlantic Coast (Articles 1 to 14)
(Unofficial translation)

Article 1

This Statute establishes the system of autonomy for the regions inhabited by the communities of the Atlantic Coast and recognizes their rights and obligations in accordance with the political Constitution.

Article 2

The communities of the Atlantic Coast are an inseparable part of the unitary and indivisible State of Nicaragua. They have the same rights and obligations as the other communities of Nicaragua.

Article 5

Spanish is the official language of the State and the languages of the Atlantic Coast communities shall be used officially in the autonomous regions.

Article 6

Two regions are established.

Article 7

Each region is divided into municipalities, the subdivision of which shall be established and organized by the regional councils according to their traditions.

Article 8

Powers of the regional governments

The autonomous regions established by this Statute are legal persons under public law which follow national policies, orientations and plans. Through their respective administrations, they have the following powers:

1. Participate in the preparation and implementation of national development plans and programs for their regions, with a view to harmonizing them with the interests of the Atlantic Coast communities;

2. Administer programs of health, education, culture, procurement, transportation and communal services, etc., in co-ordination with the Ministries concerned;

3. Instigate their own economic, social and cultural projects;

4. Promote the rational use, enjoyment and usufruct of waters, forests and communal lands, as well as the defence of their ecological system;

5. Promote the study, blossoming, preservation and dissemination of the traditional cultures of the Atlantic Coast communities, as well as their historical, artistic, linguistic and cultural heritage;

6. Promote the national culture in the Atlantic Coast communities;

7. Encourage traditional exchanges among the nations and peoples of the Caribbean, while respecting national laws and the appropriate mechanisms;

8. Promote the articulation of intraregional and interregional markets, thus contributing to the consolidation of the national market;

9. Establish regional taxes in accordance with the laws concerned.

Structures of the regional governments

The Regional Council

The Regional Council is made up of 45 members elected by universal suffrage for a four-year term. All the ethnic communities of the region must be represented on this Council (Article 19). The three deputies elected to the National Assembly from the region are ex officio members of the Regional Council (Article 20).

To run for an elected position, a candidate must come from the region and have resided there during the three months preceding the election or for five consecutive years, including the year preceding the election.

The Council regulates regional affairs in its fields of jurisdiction, as described in Article 8. It also prepares the budget, ensures the proper use of the special development fund, and elects the Executive Committee and the Regional Co-ordinator from among its members (Article 23).

The Executive Committee of the Regional Council

The Executive Committee consists of a President, two Vice-Presidents, two Secretaries and two ordinary members for a two-year term (Article 27). All ethnic communities of the region must be represented on this Committee. It co-ordinates activities with the Regional Co-ordinator and appoints standing or special committees to analyze and prepare decrees on the administration of the region's affairs.

The Regional Co-ordinator

The Regional Co-ordinator is responsible for executive functions and represents the region.

Composition of the Regional Councils following the 1990 elections

Northern Region

45 (members)
+ 3 (deputies to the National Assembly in Managua) = 48

Yatama:	23
FSLN:	22
UNO:	3

Southern Region

$45 + 3 = 48^1$

UNO:	23
FSLN:	18
Yatama:	4

Composition of the Regional Councils following the 1994 elections

Northern Region

45 members

FSLN:	19
PLC^2:	19
Yatama:	7

Southern Region

45 members

PLC:	18
FSLN:	14
UNO:	5
Yatama:	5
MAAC:	2
ADECO:	1

Notes

1. The three deputies are not included in the available data. (*Envio,* June 1991).
2. PLC: Constitutional Liberal Party; MAAC *Movimiento Auténtico Autonómo Costeño: ADECO; Alianza Democrática Costeña.*

Appendix IV

General Data and Living Conditions in Nicaragua's Northern Atlantic Autonomous Region

General data[1]

Population: 160,376 (1991 figures).

Maternal mortality: 38.4 per 10,000 live births.

Active population: 60,300, or 39.6% of the population (1989). About 60% are agricultural producing, 27% engage in artisanal fishing, 8% work in artisanal or industrial mines and 5% live from forest activities.

Average unemployment rate: between 60 and 70%.

Education: some 150 schools can meet 83% of the needs for the first four years of primary school. Only 12% of pupils can complete primary school and half of these can go on to secondary school. Four technical schools can accommodate 685 students.

Medical personnel: 32 doctors and 343 nurses in 1989.

Living conditions

Interview with the Miskito Sandinista deputy Myrna Cunningham, conducted in October 1992.

Health: "The level of health has declined considerably in the past two years. Half the clinics we had are now closed because of a lack of medicines and medical staff. They have left the region because of economic measures instituted by the government. There is an increase in malaria, tuberculosis and diseases which had practically disappeared before 1990. There is also an increase in the malnutrition rate among children under five years of age. Some people who had been refugees in Honduras have returned with tuberculosis or diseases that we didn't have here."

Education: "We have a lot of problems with regard to education. In the region, nearly 10,000 children could not go to school this year because of a lack of teachers and because some schools were not open.

But the most serious problem is that our bilingual education program, which was created in 1984, has suffered from the central government's budget restrictions. This week, it laid off the rest of the workers. It initially tried to eliminate this type of program in the Sumu and Miskito regions.

"The other problem is that students who graduate from secondary school cannot go to Managua to study at the university. We are trying to open our own universities on the Coast, but we do not have enough financial support from the central government. The majority of students therefore do not complete their studies. Of 500 students who completed secondary school in 1991, only seven could go to Managua."

Transportation: "Puerto Cabezas is nearly 700 kilometres from Managua. It takes several hours to get from Puerto Cabezas to any community. The roads are in lamentable condition. The road is impracticable between Puerto Cabezas and the mining region. This means that basic products are extremely expensive when they reach Puerto Cabezas. Even if people manage to plant rice and beans, the poor condition of the roads prevents them from selling them, since nobody can come to buy them. They have to send them to Honduras where access is easier. Nicaragua then will import these products at a higher price. It's the people who lose out."

Note

1. CAPRI, op. cit., Centro Humbolt, 1992, pp. 109-118.

Appendix V
Ethnic Groups of Colombia

The main ethnic groups of Colombian society are the Blacks, the indigenous peoples and the Natives of the San Andrés Islands.

The country probably has 3 million Blacks,[1] or 10 percent of the population. Inhabiting the Atlantic and Pacific Coasts and the downstream areas of the Cauca and Magdalena Rivers of the Andes, most Blacks are integrated into national society. Some live in the big cities; however, even among urban dwellers, their own cultural expressions can be distinguished. This is explained by the history of their arrival in America, in a complete uprooting from their environment. In the following years, they never had the leeway to reconstitute a territory or a culture. It was only with the Maroon rebellions of the 17th and 18th centuries that Black communities split off from the slaveholding cities and large farms to begin their own process of ethnic identification. This process, which has continued to this day, has been recognized for the first time by the new Constitution.

There are about 600,000 indigenous people, or 2 percent of the population. Belonging to 82 different peoples, they are distributed throughout Colombia. Thanks to their tenacious struggle, they have managed to keep some land, their usage and customs, their languages, a social organization and a cultural identity. For legal purposes, they are organized into *resguardos* and governed by councils under Law 89 of 1890. The preamble of this law states that the country's general legislation does not apply to "savages, who diminish civilization." But one way or another, it is this law which became the focus for the dynamic processes of organization and recovery of indigenous lands and culture. Most indigenous peoples are now part of the National Organization of Indigenous Peoples of Colombia (ONIC).

The Natives of the San Andrés and Providencia Archipelago, located 700 kilometres from the Atlantic Coast, constitute an ethnic group with clearly defined characteristics. The result of Black and White migrations from nearby islands in the 17th century, they in turn have been part of the Viceroyalty of New Grenada, Greater Colombia and finally the Republic of Colombia. As exclusive owners of the island territories for several centuries, they have developed their own culture, based on English and the Protestant religion. During this century, Colombia has experienced a twofold process of migration (from the continent to the islands) and acculturation of the Natives. By displacing them from their territories, the viability of the islands' resources has been imperilled.

Note

1. The demographic estimate of different ethnic groups in Colombia is still approximate and varies considerably depending on the source. The very definitions of Black and indigenous people are changeable. These figures are therefore indicative. For the indigenous population, The ONIC authors themselves use two figures, 600,000 and 800,000. The first refers to the official estimates, which put them at about 2 percent of the Colombian population, and the second refers to an estimated of persons who call themselves indigenous. No census confirms the accuracy of either of these figures.

The Rights of Indigenous Peoples and Other Ethnic Groups in the New Colombian Constitution

Fundamental principles

1. The State recognizes that the Colombian nation is multiethnic and pluricultural (Article 7).

2. The State recognizes the equality and dignity of all cultures which live together in Colombia (Article 70).

Right to culture

1. The languages and dialects of ethnic groups are official in their territories; schooling in these territories therefore must be bilingual (Article 10).

2. Education of ethnic groups must respect and develop their cultural identity (Article 68).

Right to property

1. The *resguardos* are collective property (Article 329); they cannot be sold, seized or abandoned (Article 63).

2. The communal lands of ethnic groups are reserved (Article 63). The ownership by Black communities of their ancestral possessions is recognized (transitional Article 55) and controls will be implemented to protect the Natives of the San Andrés Archipelago (Article 310 and transitional Article 42).

3. The rights of ethnic groups to the zones of archaeological wealth are guaranteed (Article 72).

4. The exploitation of natural resources in the territories of indigenous peoples must be done with their participation and with respect for their culture, society and economy (Article 329). This right extends to the construction of public works (judgement of the Constitutional Court, June 24, 1992).

Right to autonomy

1. The indigenous territories are territorial entities endowed with autonomy and the right to their own government, specific functions, their own resources and national transfer payments (Article 286 and 287). After consultation with the communities, the law will specify what will be included in the Indigenous Territorial Entities (ETI); the territorial limits will then be defined (Article 329 and transitional Article 56).
2. The ETIs will be governed by councils, the composition of which will be ensured by the communities according to their customs and which will assume responsibility for matters of settlement, development plans, public investments, natural resources and public order, among other functions (Article 330).

Right to jurisdiction

The indigenous peoples may exercise judicial functions in their territory (Article 246).

Right to political representation

1. The indigenous peoples are entitled to at least two positions in the Senate of the Republic (Article 171).
2. The ethnic groups have special quotas in the House of Representatives (Article 176).

Right to financial resources

1. The Congress will decide which *resguardos* will be entitled to national transfer payments (Article 357 and transitional Article 45).
2. When the ETIs are created, they will have various sources of financing (Articles 287, 295, 330, 357 and 361).

Rights to nationality

Any individual member of indigenous peoples in border areas has the right to dual citizenship (Article 96).

Article VII

The Population of Panama

According to the 1990 census, Panama has 2,329,000 inhabitants, 194,269 of whom are indigenous people divided among three main groups: the Ngöbe-Bugles, also called Guaymis (123,626), the Kunas (47,298) and the Embera-Waunans, also known as Chocos (about 20,000 people). In addition, a few hundred Bri-Bris live along the border with Costa Rica and a few thousand Teribes in the eastern part of the Republic.

Powers of the Kuna General Congress According to the Draft Basic Law of the Kuna Yala *Comarca* (Article 14)

(Unofficial translation)

a) Dictate the measures necessary for the progress and development of the *Comarca*;

b) Analyze, approve or disapprove, and implement programs, plans and projects for development of the *Comarca* which have been submitted for its consideration;

c) Apply sanctions or coercive measures against institutions or persons who, without its authorization, carry out projects, programs and plans which have significant repercussions on the social, cultural, religious and economic order of the *Comarca*;

d) Ensure the conservation of the collective and individual property of the *Comarca*;

e) Require reports from the *sayladummagan*, committees, public and private institutions, deputies, district representative (*corregimiento*), executive or private persons when the interests of the *Comarca* so require;

f) Establish the list of candidates for the position of representative of the executive authority;

g) Elect or dismiss *sayladummagan*, according to the instructions of the Cultural General Congress, in accordance with the standards it establishes for this purpose;

h) Evaluate the activities of the *sayladummagan*;

i) Appoint work and study committees, or for any other activity it wishes to carry out;

j) Oversee the funds of the *Comarca*, regardless of their source, internal or external, and the funds allocated in the Panamanian national budget for development programs;

k) Defend and preserve the territorial integrity and identity of the people, both within and outside the *Comarca*;

l) Ensure preservation of the ecosystem and rational use of natural resources;

m) Penalize the *sayladummagan* when they do not fulfil their functions or exceed their jurisdiction, or for offences against moral

standards or the provisions of the Congress as established in the
Statute;

n) Penalize communities and individuals who violate or fail to apply
the provisions issued by the Congress;

o) Agree on contracts with the national government or with other national and international agencies or private persons.

Excerpts from the 1988 Brazilian Constitution[1]
(unofficial translation)

Title III. On the Organization of the State

Chapter II. On the Union

Art. 20. The following are considered to be property of the Union:

 xi. lands traditionally occupied by Indians.

Art. 22. The Union has exclusive jurisdiction to legislate on:

 xiv. the indigenous populations.

Title IV. On the Organization of Powers

Chapter II. On the Legislative Branch

Section II. Powers of the National Congress

Art. 49. The National Congress has exclusive jurisdiction to:

 xvi. authorize the exploitation of water resources, prospecting and mining of mineral wealth on the indigenous lands.

Chapter III. On the Judicial Branch

Art. 109. Federal judges have jurisdiction in trials and judgments relating to:

 xi. disputes on indigenous rights.

Chapter IV. On the Essential Functions of Justice

Section 1. On the Public Ministry

Art. 129. The Public Ministry has the institutional functions:

 v. of defending the rights of interests of the indigenous populations.

Title VII. On the Economic and Financial Order

Chapter I. On the general principles of economic activity

Art. 176. Mineral deposits, whether exploited or not, and other mineral resources, as well as hydraulic energy sources, have ownership distinct from the soil, for the purposes of their exploitation, and belong to the Union, with the licence holder being guaranteed ownership of the proceeds of their exploitation.

1. Prospecting and exploitation of the mineral resources and energy sources to which the *caput* of this article refers may only be done upon authorization of concession by the Union, in the interest of the nation, by Brazilians or Brazilian companies with national capital, according to the law which shall establish specific conditions when these activities are conducted in border areas or on indigenous lands.

Title VIII. On the Social Order

Chapter III. On education, culture and sports

Section I. On education

Art. 210, 2. Regular basic instruction shall be given in the Portuguese language, with the indigenous communities being guaranteed the use of their mother tongues and their own learning processes.

Section II. On culture

Art. 215, 1. The State shall protect manifestations of popular, indigenous and Afro-Brazilian culture, and those of other groups who participate in the national cultural process.

Chapter VIII. On Indians

Art. 231. The social organization, customs, languages, beliefs, traditions and original rights of Indians on the lands they traditionally occupy are recognized, the Union being bound to proceed with demarcation of these lands and to protect and enforce respect for all their property.

1. The lands traditionally occupied by Indians are those which they inhabit permanently, those which they use for their productive activities, those which are indispensable to the preservation of the resources of the natural environment necessary for their well-being and those which are necessary for their physical and cultural reproduction according to their usages, customs and traditions.

2. The lands traditionally occupied by Indians are intended for their permanent possession, with the right of use of the wealth of the soil, watercourses and lakes being reserved for them exclusively.

3. The use of water resources, including energy potential, prospecting and exploitation of mineral wealth on indigenous lands may only be realized with the authorization of the National Congress, the affected communities being consulted and their participation in the proceeds of this exploitation assured according to the terms established by law.

4. The lands mentioned in this article are inalienable and unavailable and the rights to them are indefeasible.

5. The displacement of indigenous groups from their lands is prohibited, except *ad referendum* of the National Congress, in case of catastrophes or epidemics which endanger their population, or in the interest of the country's sovereignty, after deliberation of the National Congress, their immediate return being guaranteed, no matter what the hypothetical situation, once the risk is gone.

6. Acts with the object of occupation, ownership and possession of the lands to which this article pertains or exploitation of the natural wealth of the soil, watercourses and lakes found therein, are null and void, producing no legal effect, with the exception of those concerning the public interest of the Union, as will be provided in a complementary law, the annulment and extinction of these acts not giving rise to any right of compensation or

recourse against the Union, except, under the terms of the law, for investments resulting from occupation in good faith.

7. The provisions of Article 174, nos 3 and 4 do not apply to indigenous lands.[2]

Art. 232. Indians, their communities and their organizations are legitimate parties to appear in court in the defence of their rights and interests, the Public Ministry being bound to intervene in all the records of the trial.

Act under transitional constitutional provisions

Art. 67. The union will conclude the acts of demarcation of indigenous lands within five years of the proclamation of the Constitution.

Notes

1. Taken from Bruce Albert, op. cit., p. 15.
2. This alludes to the precedence given to gold prospecting co-operatives to obtain mining concessions in the zones they exploited before the proclamation of the Constitution.

Also published by

A NATION WITHIN A NATION
Dependency and the Cree
Marie-Anik Gagné

Strongly opposed to abstract theories of social evolutionism, this book eloquently argues that First Nations have been forcibly brought into the orbit of world capitalism via "imperialization." This has caused their economic subjection and oppression where freedom and strength could have been. As a direct result, the First Nations have become dependant, "underdeveloped," and lacking in self-reliance. Gagné argues compellingly against assimilation and for co-operation and power-sharing within a forum of respect and good faith.

168 pages, index, maps
Paperback ISBN: 1-551640-12-0 $19.99
Hardcover ISBN: 1-551640-13-9 $38.99

ELECTRIC RIVERS
The Story of the James Bay Project
Sean McCutcheon

The first complete and fair-minded account of one of the most controversial environmental issues of our time.

...a book about how and why the James Bay project is being built, how it works, the consequences its building will have for people and for the environment, and the struggle to stop it...it cuts through the rhetoric so frequently found in the debate.
Canadian Book Review Annual

194 pages, maps
Paperback ISBN: 1-895431-18-2 $18.99
Hardcover ISBN: 1-895431-19-0 $37.99

THE NEW RESOURCE WARS
Native Struggles Against Multinational Corporations
Al Gedicks

Aboriginal and environmental coalitions fighting against corporate greed and environmental racism is mirrored in hundreds of struggles all over the world, from James Bay, Québec to the Ecuadorian Amazon Rainforest. This new book documents these struggles and explores the underlying motivations and social forces that propel them. It concludes with a discussion of Native treaty rights and the next stage of the environmental movement.

250 pages, index
Paperback ISBN: 1-551640-00-7 $19.99
Hardcover ISBN: 1-551640-01-5 $38.99

WOLLASTON

People Resisting Genocide

Miles Goldstick

Foreword by Dr. Rosalie Bertell

The story of the Natives' struggle in northern Saskatchewan to protect their homes from the effects of uranium mining.

These are important issues, and in raising them Goldstick does us a service.

Border/Lines

315 pages, photographs, illustrations
Paperback ISBN: 0-920057-95-0 $16.99
Hardcover ISBN: 0-920057-94-2 $36.99

POLITICAL ECOLOGY

Beyond Environmentalism

Dimitrios Roussopoulos

Examining the perspective offered by various components of political ecology, this book presents an overview of its origins as well as its social and cultural causes, and summarizes the differences, and similarities, between political ecology and social ecology.

180 pages
Paperback ISBN: 1-895431-80-8 $15.99
Hardcover ISBN: 1-895431-81-6 $34.99

GREEN POLITICS

Agenda For a Free Society

Dimitrios Roussopoulos

An international survey of various Green political parties is presented, featuring their programmes and progress. The result is a stimulating book that challenges accepted ideas about how the world should be organized, and suggests the possibility of a safe and more satisfying future.

200 pages, index
Paperback ISBN: 0-921689-74-8 $19.99
Hardcover ISBN: 0-921689-75-6 $38.99

FROM THE GROUND UP

Essays on Grassroots and Workplace Democracy

C. George Benello

Len Krimerman, Frank Lindenfeld, Carol Korty & Julian Benello, eds.

Foreword by Dimitrios Roussopoulos

George Benello argues that modern social movements need to rise to the challenge of spearheading a radical reorganization of society based on the principles of decentralization, community control, and participatory democracy.

251 pages, index
Paperback ISBN: 1-895431-32-8 $19.99
Hardcover ISBN: 1-895431-33-6 $38.99

COMMUNICATION
For and Against Democracy
Marc Raboy and Peter A. Bruck, eds.

These pieces...do much to increase reader awareness of the increasing "mediatization" of society, the role of communications in global politics and economics, social experimentation with communication practices in national settings, and the strengths and limitation of mass communication instruments as "facilitators of democracy".
Choice

248 pages
Paperback ISBN: 0-921689-46-2 $19.99
Hardcover ISBN: 0-921689-47-0 $39.99

COMMON CENTS
Media Portrayal of the Gulf War and Other Events
James Winter

Objectivity is the theme of these five case studies which deal with how the media covered the Gulf War, the Oka standoff, the Ontario NDP's budget, the Meech Lake Accord and Free Trade. Winter shows how media coverage of events consistently casts them in what becomes a seemingly apolitical 'common-sense' framework, a framework which actually represents the opinions of the power elite.

Winter provides strong evidence of a corporate tilt in the mass media...it is impossible to dismiss [his] arguments.
Vancouver Sun

Like Chomsky, he enjoys contrasting the "common-sense" interpretation with views from alternative sources. As facts and images clash, we end up with a better grasp of the issues at hand.
Montréal Gazette

304 pages, index
Paperback ISBN: 1-895431-24-7 $23.99
Hardcover ISBN: 1-895431-25-5 $42.99

VIDEO THE CHANGING WORLD
Nancy Thede and Alain Ambrosi, eds.

An international collection of articles which explore the variety of initiatives that have emerged the world over in the past decade, and the internal debates.

A welcome contribution to the scant literature on the role of marginalized media in social communication.
Canadian Book Review Annual

This collection...identifies and gives a platform to active and activist video organizations...and sketches the ideological stance of grass-roots communications technologies as agents of democratic development.
Journal of Communications

224 pages
Hardcover ISBN: 1-895431-03-4 $37.99